Differentiating for Inclusion

Target Ladders:
Dyslexia

Kate Ruttle

LDA has a range of learning development aids to help children with special needs and general learning difficulties. For our full range and helpful information, visit www.ldalearning.com.

Permission to photocopy

This book contains materials which may be reproduced by photocopier or other means for use by the purchaser. The permission is granted on the understanding that these copies will be used within the educational establishment of the purchaser. The book and all its contents remain copyright. Copies may be made without reference to the publisher or the licensing scheme for the making of photocopies operated by the Publishers' Licensing Agency.

The right of Kate Ruttle to be identified as the author of this work has been asserted by her in accordance with sections 77 and 78 of the Copyright, Designs and Patents Act of 1988.

Target Ladders: Dyslexia

ISBN 978-1-85503-548-5

© Kate Ruttle 2013

Contains public sector information licensed under the Open Government Licence v1.0.

All Rights Reserved

First published 2013

Reprinted 2014, 2015

Printed in the UK for LDA

LDA, Findel Education, Hyde Buildings, Ashton Road, Hyde, Cheshire, SK14 4SH

Contents

Introduction: Closing the gap   4

Using Target Ladders
How to use this book   6
Scope and Sequence charts   11
Records of Progress   19

Dyslexia
What is dyslexia?   23
Dyslexia indicators   25
How can I get a diagnosis – and what can I do to help?   27
What dyslexic learners find hard   29
The dyslexia-friendly classroom   34
Dyslexia and numeracy   38

The Target Ladders
Aspect 1: Phonological awareness   40
Aspect 2: Visual and auditory perception and memory   48
Aspect 3: Phonics and spelling   56
Aspect 4: Reading comprehension and fluency   64
Aspect 5: Writing – handwriting, punctuation, sentences and text   72
Aspect 6: Planning, organising and remembering   80
Aspect 7: Self-confidence and motivation   88

Links to other *Target Ladders* titles   96
Other useful resources from LDA   96

Closing the gap

Although schools are trying to reduce the number of children on their Special Educational Need (SEN) registers, the array of learning difficulties faced by the children is not changing or diminishing. In many areas, the responsibility for identifying learning difficulties, and supporting the children, is being thrust more onto schools because the external services hitherto available to support identification and remediation are fast disappearing. In most primary schools, the responsibility for tackling children's learning challenges continues to lie with class teachers and Special Educational Needs Co-ordinators (SENCos), many of whom are non-specialists.

Following the Bew Report of 2011, and with the introduction of the Phonics Screening Check in 2012, the focus for OFSTED inspections is changing from a scrutiny of the attainment of the middle and high achievers to that of the progress made by the children with the lowest attainment. Inspectors are now looking for evidence that schools are working to 'close the gap'. The first step in closing the gap is to identify what learners can already do.

Case study

Class teachers in particular often find it hard to identify targets for children. For example, a teacher gave a Year 7 child the target to *'Read with even more expression'*. A discussion with the teacher, exploring the child's strengths and weaknesses, revealed that the main problem was that the child did not make sense of what she read. She struggled to read longer sentences with appropriate intonation, because she lost sense of the meaning, and this was what the teacher had noticed. But the target 'to read with even more expression' did not accurately pinpoint anything that was useful to the child.

Whether individual targets are recorded on an Individual Education Plan (IEP), an internal target sheet, a Record of Progress (RoP) or some other mechanism, the fact remains that these children continue to need small-steps targets in order to clarify learning priorities and give the children a sense of achievement when they tick off another target.

The *Target Ladders* titles focus on one SEN at a time, in order that the range of difficulties and challenges facing young people with that SEN can be acknowledged. A child does not, however, need to have a diagnosis in order to be helped by the targets and strategies mentioned in a book. If any child in your care has any of the behaviours or difficulties addressed by the book, then the targets listed should be helpful and appropriate.

The *Target Ladders* books aim to support you in the following ways:

- Focusing on what a child can do, rather than what they cannot do, in order to identify next steps.
- Presenting 'small-steps' targets for children.
- Suggesting strategies and activities you may find helpful in order to achieve the targets.
- Linking attainment to P scales and National Curriculum levels wherever relevant. (Please ignore these links if you work outside England.)
- Giving you the information you need to use your professional judgement and understanding of the child in determining priorities for learning.
- Recognising that every child is different and will follow their own pathway through the targets.
- Giving you an overview of the range of difficulties experienced by children with a particular SEN. Not all children will experience all of the difficulties, but once you know and understand the implications of the SEN, it gives you a better understanding as to a child's learning priorities.
- Providing a system for setting and monitoring targets which can replace or complement IEPs.

Setting useful targets for a child can be tricky. But *'he can't do anything'* is not a constructive statement when deciding what the next steps should be. In order to support the child, you need to find out first what they can do already. Once you know this, you are in a good position to set targets and consider interventions.

Case study

A Year 2 teacher was concerned because a child had not made progress in his reading. *'He can't read!'* she said. When asked what the child *could* do, her response was *'Lots of things, but he can't read!'* Further discussions about whether or not the child could match, sequence, make patterns, sort letters, remember instructions, and so on elicited the recognition that the teacher wasn't aware that any of these skills are precursors to reading. Therefore, she would not have thought of setting them as targets.

It often seems easier to differentiate an activity rather than the learning objective. It appears to be more inclusive, because it means that the young person with learning difficulties works with a teaching assistant and completes the same activities as the rest of the class. However, this approach to inclusion does nothing to address the underlying learning difficulties and may contribute to teaching children to be dependent on adult help.

Using the *Target Ladders* books will enable both non-specialist teachers and SENCos to identify appropriate learning goals for independent learning, to adapt the suggested strategies or ideas for their own pupils, and to begin to make an impact on the learning difficulty and to close the gap.

How to use this book

You will find a simple five-step summary of how to use this book on page 9.

Every dyslexic child has different strengths and weaknesses. The priority for addressing these will be determined by the difficulties currently being faced by the child and will depend on your professional judgement, informed by the child's current anxieties.

In order to support you with focused target-setting, the book is structured as follows:

- Seven different Aspects of dyslexia have been identified (see Fig. 1 opposite). Think about the child's difficulties: which of these Aspects is causing most concern at the moment?
- Within each Aspect there are four different Target Ladders, each based on a particular area of skills. This is intended to help you to think carefully about precisely where the barrier may be.
- The relevant Target Ladder can then be used to identify the 'next step' target for the child.
- Suggested activities offer classroom-friendly ideas so you can support the child to meet their target.

For example, as you can see in the chart opposite, difficulties with Aspect 2: Visual and auditory perception and memory, are subdivided into four Target Ladders: Visual perception, Visual memory, Auditory perception and Auditory memory. Each Target Ladder contains up to 28 targets.

Aspects, Target Ladders and Targets

Aspects

The seven different Aspects of dyslexia identified in this book are all commonly found in children who have dyslexia, although not all of them may seem to relate immediately to difficulties with reading and writing, and not all children experience the same difficulties. You will find some helpful general guidance on teaching children with dyslexia on pages 23–39, but for more detailed information, please see books devoted to the subject, for example, *How to Identify and Support Children with Dyslexia* (Chris Neanon, LDA 2002).

The mastery of all of the identified Aspects of dyslexia (or any other SEN) is important in order that a child can learn the range of strategies they need to overcome their difficulties, improve their performance and gain confidence. The priority when deciding which of the Aspects is most important is an analysis of the individual child's current skills.

The Aspects of dyslexia identified in this book are:

1. Phonological awareness
2. Visual and auditory perception and memory
3. Phonics and spelling
4. Reading comprehension and fluency
5. Writing – handwriting, punctuation, sentences and text
6. Planning, organising and remembering
7. Self-confidence and motivation.

Target Ladders

Each of the Aspects is further subdivided into four Target Ladders, each of which addresses different parts of the Aspect (see Fig. 1). These enable you to develop your understanding of the child's individual learning needs, 'drilling down' to assist you to identify the child's particular strengths and weaknesses. The Target Ladders are set out on pages 40–95.

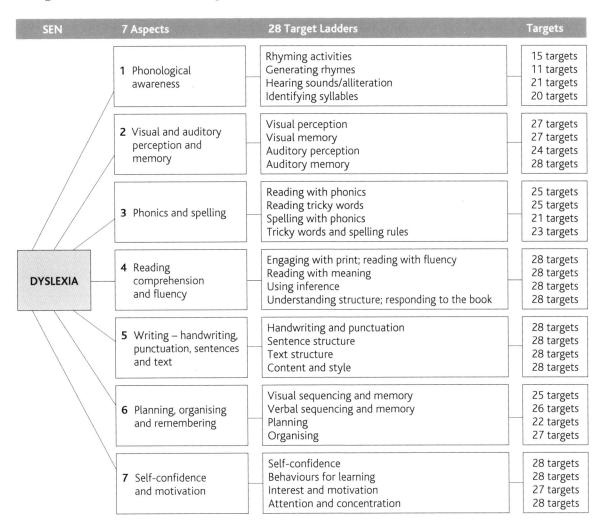

Fig. 1: The structure of *Target Ladders: Dyslexia*. Each of the seven Aspects of dyslexia has four Target Ladders, each with up to 28 small-steps targets.

How to use this book 7

Targets

There are up to 28 targets in each Target Ladder, with the simplest labelled with the letter 'A', then moving through the alphabet up to 'N', which are the most difficult. Pairs of targets, identified by the same letter, present a similar level of challenge. So, for example, all of the targets marked 'E' are at approximately the same level of development, which is slightly easier than F and slightly harder than D. Since each child is individual, some children will achieve harder targets before they do easier ones – and no child would be expected to work their way through all of the targets.

Where appropriate, a National Curriculum level, including P scales, is also shown. This is a broad guide to the level that the target feeds into.

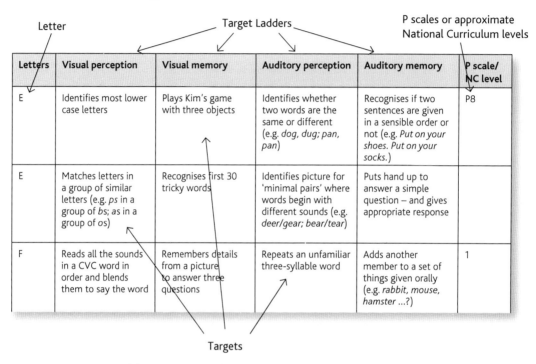

Fig. 2: Part of the Target Ladders table for Aspect 2: Visual and auditory perception and memory (page 50), showing how targets are structured in the ladders and how 'Letters' relate to National Curriculum levels.

However, it is not necessarily the case that the targets in row E for every Aspect are at the same developmental level, because the Aspects are so different. Thus, a child may have a target from row E in Aspect 3: Phonics and spelling, but a target from row H in Aspect 2: Visual and auditory perception and memory.

The targets are all written in positive language. This is to support you when you:

- look through them to find out what the child *can already* do;
- use them as the basis of the target you set for the child.

As you track the statements through each ladder, identifying what the child can already do, be aware of missed steps. If a child has missed one of the steps, further progress up that ladder may be insecure. Many children learn to mask the missed step, using developing skills in other areas to help them, but the time may come when the missed step will cause difficulties.

Activities and strategies to achieve the targets

In the Target Ladders tables on pages 40–95, targets are listed on left-hand pages. The corresponding right-hand pages offer ideas for activities and strategies that you might use to help to achieve the targets. These are suggestions only – but they have all been used successfully in classrooms. Many of the activities listed are accepted good practice and are recommended in most books about dyslexia. Here, however, the activities are shown at the point in the developmental process at which they are likely to make the most impact.

The suggested activities can often be adapted to work for a range of targets within this stage of the ladder. For this reason, activities are generally not linked to individual targets.

How to set targets: A five-step summary

1. Use Fig. 1 on page 7 to identify the one or two Aspects of dyslexia that are most troublesome for the child.

2. Turn to the Scope and Sequence charts on pages 11–18. These charts will help you pinpoint the specific targets you need – a more detailed explanation is given on page 11. The Scope and Sequence charts show the *upper limit* of the targets reached in each Target Ladder in each Aspect. Use these to gain an indication of where in the book you are likely to find appropriate targets.

3. In the Target Ladders tables on pages 40–95, locate the targets that you have identified from the Scope and Sequence charts and pinpoint specific ones for the child to work towards.

4. Photocopy or print out from the CD the relevant targets page so that you can:
   - highlight and date those the child can already do;
   - identify the next priorities.

5. Use the Record of Progress sheet on page 20 to create a copy of the targets for the child or their parents.

Making the most of Target Ladders

You may find the following tips helpful when setting your targets.

- If you are not sure which Aspect to highlight for a child:
  - think about your main concerns about that child's learning;
  - talk to the child about what they would like to improve;
  - discuss targets with the child's parents/carers.

A target that the child wants to improve is more likely to be successful.

- Once you have identified the Aspect, use the Scope and Sequence charts on pages 12–18 to identify the most beneficial Target Ladder and to ascertain which page to start on.
    - First look for any 'missed steps', and target those first. The child is likely to find success fairly quickly and will be motivated to continue to try to reach new targets.
    - Talk to the child and agree an appropriate target based on your skills inventory. Again, targets that the child is aware of tend to be achieved most quickly and are motivational.
- The target does not have to be the lowest unachieved statement in any ladder: use your professional judgement and knowledge of the child to identify the most useful and important target for the child.
- No child will follow all of the targets in precisely the order listed. Use your professional judgement, and your knowledge about what the child can already do, to identify the most appropriate target and be realistic in your expectations. There may be some zigzagging up and down a column.
- When setting targets, always ask yourself practical questions:
    - What can I change in order to enable the child to meet the targets?
    - Which people and resources are available to support the child?
    - Which skills sets am I planning to teach to the group or the whole class next?
    - What is the likelihood of a child achieving a target within the next month or so?
    - Which targets have been agreed with other children in the class?

It is important that the targets you set are realistic considering the time, the adult support and the resources available.

Once you have identified what the child can already achieve, continue to highlight and update the sheets each time the child achieves a new target. Celebrate progress with the child – while, at the same time, constantly checking to ensure that previously achieved targets remain secure. If any target becomes insecure, revise the skill briefly, without setting a formal target, in order to give the child an opportunity to consolidate the skill without feeling that they are going backwards in their achievements.

Scope and Sequence charts

The Scope and Sequence charts can be used to help you to pinpoint targets, following the advice on the preceding pages. Once you have identified the Aspect(s) you wish to focus on:

1. Find the relevant page in the Scope and Sequence charts on pages 12–18. Look for the Aspect name here:

2. Identify the Target Ladder(s) that matches the skills you wish to target. Look for the names of the ladders here:

3. Read down the list of targets here: The targets shown here are the highest for the ladder on that page. If the first target listed is too easy, look at the next target beneath it. Continue down the list until you reach a target that is beyond the child's current attainment.

4. Turn to the page number, shown here: Read all the targets on that page. One of them should be appropriate. If not, turn to the previous or subsequent page.

Scope and Sequence Aspect 2: Visual and auditory perception and memory

Visual perception

Page	Letters	Target Ladder focus	Focus of suggested activities
48	A–D	Groups objects by two parameters	Identifying an image from seeing only part of it
50	E–H	Finds five differences in detail between two similar pictures	Scotopic sensitivity/Irlen syndrome Sorting letters
52	I–L	Reads all through a long word, identifying syllable boundaries	Estimating quantity by scanning with eyes only
54	M–N	Estimates appropriately up to 50 objects	Strategies for spelling

Visual memory

Page	Letters	Target Ladder focus	Focus of suggested activities
48	A–D	Reproduces from memory a sequence of three images	Kim's game
50	E–H	Recognises 100 high-frequency words	
52	I–L	Spells longer words by chunking them into syllables	Remembering orientation of symbols
54	M–N	Copies paragraphs from cards	Accurate copying

Fig. 3: Part of the Scope and Sequence chart for Aspect 2 (see p. 13).

Bear in mind the following:

- The wording of the target may not be precisely accurate for your child. Modify it to make it appropriate.
- Different children may meet the target statements in a slightly different order. The order shown is approximate and true for many children. Adapt the order in which you set the targets for the individual child.
- No child is expected to have all of the targets on the page. A range of small-steps targets is shown in order to give you the widest possible variety of targets from which to select.
- If you cannot find a target which meets your needs, use the other targets to give you an idea of the level expected, and write your own target. It is important that all of the targets on the Record of Progress are appropriate for the individual child.

Scope and Sequence Aspect 1: Phonological awareness

Rhyming activities

Page	Letters	Target Ladder focus	Focus of suggested activities
40	A–D	Participates in rhyming activities	Vocabulary check – vocabulary for phonics (*beginning, end, start*)
42	E–H	Recites and joins in with rhymes and songs	Reciting rhymes
44	J	Uses rime and rhymes to remember curriculum facts	Curriculum rhymes

Generating rhymes

Page	Letters	Target Ladder focus	Focus of suggested activities
40	A–D	Recognises rhyme	Playing with rhyme
42	E–H	Generates rhymes for monosyllabic words	Understanding sounds, Generating rhymes
44	I–J	Groups rhyming words	Curriculum rhymes

Hearing sounds/alliteration

Page	Letters	Target Ladder focus	Focus of suggested activities
40	A–D	Repeats heard sounds	Tongue-twisters
42	E–H	Hears all three sounds in a consonant-vowel-consonant (CVC) word	Understanding sounds, Eye-Spy
44	I–L	Mentally replaces a phoneme in a CVC word	Using phonic fingers to blend and segment Phoneme replacement activities
46	M	Explains how words can be changed into other words	Changing a word

Identifying syllables

Page	Letters	Target Ladder focus	Focus of suggested activities
40	A–D	Claps syllables in a two- or three-syllable word	Copying patterns of body percussion
42	E–H	Says the number of syllables in a word	
44	I–K	Mentally replaces the first or last syllable in a two- or three-syllable word	Splitting compound words
46	M	Mentally replaces the middle syllable in a three-syllable word	Identifying syllable boundaries

Scope and Sequence Aspect 2: Visual and auditory perception and memory

Visual perception

Page	Letters	Target Ladder focus	Focus of suggested activities
48	A–D	Groups objects by two parameters	Identifying an image from seeing only part of it
50	E–H	Finds five differences in detail between two similar pictures	Scotopic sensitivity/Irlen syndrome Sorting letters
52	I–L	Reads all through a long word, identifying syllable boundaries	Estimating quantity by scanning with eyes only
54	M–N	Estimates appropriately up to 50 objects	Strategies for spelling

Visual memory

Page	Letters	Target Ladder focus	Focus of suggested activities
48	A–D	Reproduces from memory a sequence of three images	Kim's game
50	E–H	Recognises 100 high-frequency words	
52	I–L	Spells longer words by chunking them into syllables	Remembering orientation of symbols
54	M–N	Copies paragraphs from cards	Accurate copying

Auditory perception

Page	Letters	Target Ladder focus	Focus of suggested activities
48	A–D	Identifies whether two similar sounds are the same	Auditory lotto
50	E–H	Blends three heard syllables to say a word	Identifying minimal pairs
52	I–L	Reads and pronounces two- to three-syllable words accurately	'Take-up time'
54	M–N	Follows instructions at the same time as peers	Mind mapping

Auditory memory

Page	Letters	Target Ladder focus	Focus of suggested activities
48	A–D	Carries a simple message to a familiar classroom	'Simon Says'
50	E–H	Knows number bonds of 10	Active listening Riddles
52	I–L	Maintains focus for 15 minutes of teacher talk	Following a sequence of instructions Barrier tasks
54	M–N	Remembers all times tables	Alphabetical order

Scope and Sequence Aspect 3: Phonics and spelling

Reading with phonics

Page	Letters	Target Ladder focus	Focus of suggested activities
56	A–D	Blends to read CVC words	Multi-sensory phonics Alliterative sentences
58	E–H	Knows alternative pronunciations of common letter patterns	Reading to the end of a word
60	I–L	Tackles polysyllabic words with confidence	Digraph bingo
62	M	Uses phonic, contextual, graphic and syntactical cues	

Reading tricky words

Page	Letters	Target Ladder focus	Focus of suggested activities
56	A–D	Recognises 30 high-frequency words	Tricky words word hunt
58	E–H	Recognises 100 high-frequency words	
60	I–L	Recognises many common suffixes and prefixes	Reading syllables
62	M–N	Begins to make some use of related words when working out meanings	

Spelling with phonics

Page	Letters	Target Ladder focus	Focus of suggested activities
56	A–D	Segments and records CVC words	Dictations
58	E–H	Writes some CVC words with long vowels	Recognising and writing graphemes Stretching words
60	I–L	Makes plausible attempts to spell less common words	Using rimes
62	M	Spells curriculum and topic words correctly	Look, say, cover, write, check Sound it out

Tricky words and spelling rules

Page	Letters	Target Ladder focus	Focus of suggested activities
56	B–D	Writes five simple words from memory	Using 'magic lines'
58	E–H	Spells up to 30 tricky words	Table top writing mats
60	I–L	Spells common grammatical function words	Long and short vowels
62	M–N	Knows common spelling rules	Spelling rules

Scope and Sequence Aspect 4: Reading comprehension and fluency

Engaging with print; reading with fluency

Page	Letters	Target Ladder focus	Focus of suggested activities
64	A–D	Points to individual words from left to right	Matching and sequencing activities
66	E–H	Begins to use expression when re-reading familiar books	Fluency and punctuation
68	I–L	Self-corrects if the reading does not make sense	Summarising
70	M–N	Reads longer texts with sustained concentration	Highlighting

Reading with meaning

Page	Letters	Target Ladder focus	Focus of suggested activities
64	A–D	'Reads back' own writing with 1–1 correspondence	
66	E–H	Answers simple questions using details from book	Making meaning
68	I–L	Identifies the main points in a paragraph	Skimming and scanning
70	M–N	Skims, scans and makes notes to support oral summary	Comprehension monitoring

Using inference

Page	Letters	Target Ladder focus	Focus of suggested activities
64	A–D	Links events in books to own experience	Inferring meaning from pictures
66	E–H	Uses pictures to identify who said what	Using inference
68	I–L	Uses relevant information from a text in research activities	Skimming and scanning
70	M–N	Finds words and phrases in the text to support interpretation of ideas	Answering comprehension questions

Understanding structure; responding to the book

Page	Letters	Target Ladder focus	Focus of suggested activities
64	A–D	Knows the sequence of events in a book	Reading as a social activity
66	E–H	Knows that some books have stories and others have information	Sequencing ideas
68	I–L	Identifies powerful words and phrases and discusses their impact	Reading e-texts
70	M–N	Uses technical vocabulary to comment on the efficacy of writing	Mind mapping

Scope and Sequence Aspect 5: Writing – handwriting, punctuation, sentences and text

Handwriting and punctuation

Page	Letters	Target Ladder focus	Focus of suggested activities
72	A–D	Begins to leave spaces between groups of letters	Pencil grip and seating Letter formation
74	E–H	Most letters correctly orientated	
76	I–L	Handwriting is consistently legible and neat	Joined writing
78	M–N	End of sentence punctuation is accurate	

Sentence structure

Page	Letters	Target Ladder focus	Focus of suggested activities
72	A–D	Orders words from left to right	
74	E–H	Sentence structures match model text	Reorganising sentences Using model texts
76	I–L	Sentences linked by a wider variety of connectives	
78	M–N	Some sentences begin with subordinate clauses	Oral work to develop sentences and language

Text structure

Page	Letters	Target Ladder focus	Focus of suggested activities
72	A–D	Retells simple familiar stories in sequence	Lines or blank paper?
74	E–H	Events and ideas are generally in an appropriate order	Remembering all the layers of text
76	I–L	Events or stages are clearly distinguished	Planning
78	M–N	Paragraphs are sometimes evident	Guided writing

Content and style

Page	Letters	Target Ladder focus	Focus of suggested activities
72	A–D	States purpose for own writing	Making writing fun
74	E–H	Writing can be mostly read without need for mediation	Talk for writing
76	I–L	Adjectives and adverbs are used to add more details	Using a laptop
78	M–N	Main features, including layout, of non-fiction text types are used	Guided writing

Scope and Sequence Aspect 6: Planning, organising and remembering

Visual sequencing and memory

Page	Letters	Target Ladder focus	Focus of suggested activities
80	A–D	Continues a visual pattern with two elements	Now and Next boards
82	E–H	Uses visual timetable	Visual timetables
84	J–L	Follows a simple map or a plan to find something	Strategies for remembering
86	M–N	Uses a mind map to record key ideas while teacher is talking	Following algorithms and remembering equations and formulae

Verbal sequencing and memory

Page	Letters	Target Ladder focus	Focus of suggested activities
80	A–D	Rote counts to 10	Remembering sequences
82	E–H	Describes or writes step-by-step instructions	Working memory
84	I–L	Summarises the information in a text, retaining order	Strategies for remembering
86	M–N	Articulates what is needed and knows the order in which to tackle tasks	Asking questions

Planning

Page	Letters	Target Ladder focus	Focus of suggested activities
80	A–D	With support, can set a goal to achieve immediately	Tidying up
82	E–H	Independently puts resources back in the right place	
84	I–L	Breaks complex tasks into smaller, achievable tasks	Taking responsibility
86	M–N	Takes pride in a task, without the need for recognition	Real opportunities for planning

Organising

Page	Letters	Target Ladder focus	Focus of suggested activities
80	A–D	Follows routines and begins to plan ahead	Planning what to write before mark-making
82	E–H	Uses visual checklists effectively	Language for learning
84	I–L	Evaluates and prioritises tasks to achieve	Learning with the whole class
86	M–N	Recognises what needs to be done and organises self and others to achieve it	Real opportunities for planning

Scope and Sequence Aspect 7: Self-confidence and motivation

Self-confidence

Page	Letters	Target Ladder focus	Focus of suggested activities
88	A–D	Says what they like and dislike doing	Looking after adults in the classroom
90	E–H	Participates in self-evaluation	Accepting praise
92	I–L	Shows resilience when identifying what has gone wrong	Personal power
94	M–N	Accurately and calmly identifies things they are good at and things they are less good at	Solution-focused approach

Behaviours for learning

Page	Letters	Target Ladder focus	Focus of suggested activities
88	A–D	Seeks support from an adult when there's a difficulty	Using timers
90	E–H	Gets on well with most children in the class	Making choices
92	I–L	Is not afraid of new things or taking on new tasks	Developing emotional literacy
94	M–N	Accommodates easily to changes in routine and different people	Solution-focused approach

Interest and motivation

Page	Letters	Target Ladder focus	Focus of suggested activities
88	A–D	Begins tasks when requested	Using timers
90	E–H	Resists the temptation to join another child's unwanted behaviour	Projecting 'self'
92	I–L	Predicts where the obstacles might be and suggests ideas to overcome them	Developing concentration
94	M–N	Gets started on tasks without delay and has the motivation to carry them through	Solution-focused approach

Attention and concentration

Page	Letters	Target Ladder focus	Focus of suggested activities
88	A–D	Follows an instruction directed at the whole class	Supporting children with attention problems
90	E–H	Talks about changes that might help them to pay better attention	Using fiddle toys
92	I–L	Shows determination to complete a task	Developing concentration
94	M–N	Is attentive, listens to the teacher and is not easily distracted from the task in hand	Solution-focused approach

Records of Progress

Creating a Record of Progress

Arrange to meet with the child and ask them first to tell you what they are good at. Record their responses on the Record of Progress (RoP). A blank form is supplied for you to copy on page 20 and on the CD. Ask the child then to tell you which areas they would most like to improve. If it is appropriate, choose something that addresses at least one of their issues as a target, so that the child feels some ownership of their RoP. If your school operates a Pupil Passport system, then you may want to amend the RoP form, but you will nonetheless need a sheet that can be annotated and amended.

As you add one or two more targets, talk to the child to check that they agree that each target is relevant and that they understand what they will need to do to achieve their targets. Targets that children do not know or care about are much harder for them to achieve. Limit the number of targets to a maximum of three. Remember, you do not need to use the precise wording of the targets given in this book: adapt the words to match the maturity and understanding of the learner.

If you are planning to use a published intervention, check to see what the recommended length of time for the intervention is. Monitor the impact of the intervention (see page 21) and review at regular intervals – at least monthly – to see if there is an impact. If not, consider whether a different intervention would be more effective.

Principles for the effective use of an RoP include the following:

- The form must be 'live'. The child will need to have access to it at all times, as will all adults who work with the child, in order that it can be referred to, amended and updated regularly. It would be good practice to send a copy home for the parents/carers. If you think that the child is likely to lose or destroy their RoP, make a photocopy so that you can supply another.
- Together with the child, you have identified their priority areas for learning. These should be addressed as often as possible, across the curriculum.
- As soon as each target has been achieved, according to the success criteria you agreed, the form should be dated and a 'next step' considered.
- When you set up the RoP, select a review date which is ideally about a month ahead and no more than half a term ahead. Don't wait until this date to identify that targets have been achieved, but on this date review progress towards all targets – or identified next steps – and agree new targets.
- If a target has not been achieved, consider why not. If possible, try a different approach to meeting the target. Having the same target over and over is likely to bore the child and put them off following their RoP.

RECORD OF PROGRESS

Name _____ Class _____ Date agreed _____ Review date _____

I am good at	My targets are	I will know that I have achieved my target when I can	Date when I achieved my target	Next steps
I would like to be better at				
It helps me when				

RoP number: _____ Targets approved by: Pupil _____ Teacher _____

SENCo _____ Parent/Carer _____ TA _____

Using Target Ladders

Monitoring a Record of Progress

In order to ensure that your Record of Progress (RoP) is used effectively, you need to monitor progress towards the targets each time you offer support. Use a monitoring sheet; a photocopiable example is given on page 22 and on the CD.

- Use a separate sheet – copied on to a different colour of paper – for each target.
- Write the child's name at the top of the sheet and the target underneath.
- On each occasion when someone works with the child towards the target, they should write the smaller, more specific target that you are working towards *during this session* in the box.
- They should then write a comment. On each occasion the child achieves the target during the session and then back in class, tick the box.

Comments should, as far as possible, refer to the child's learning rather than to their behaviour (unless it is a behaviour target). The intention is that these sheets should be used to create a cumulative record of a child's session-by-session progress towards their target. The evidence here can be used to assess the impact of an intervention in order that its appropriateness can be evaluated swiftly and any additional actions can be taken promptly. The advice is, therefore, to keep comments about attitude to a minimum (for example, you might draw a smiley face to indicate good attention) unless behaviour is impeding the learning.

What precisely you record will depend on the type of support being offered and the nature of the target.

- If you are delivering a planned intervention, make a record of the unit/page/activity and a comment about the learning the child demonstrated. For example, a comment relating to a target about the number of high-frequency words a child can read might state: '*was*, *the*, *but* are secure; *you* is still insecure'.
- If you are offering support in the classroom, you might want to comment on the child's learning over a few lessons. Focus on what the child has achieved in the lessons and whether the learning is secure.
- If you are offering support for behaviour, comment only on evidence of the behaviours listed in the target. As a general principle, aim to include more positive than negative comments, and always try to balance a negative with a positive comment.

At the monthly review of the RoP, collect together all of the monitoring sheets and look at the frequency of the comments against each target as well as the learning they reflect. If a child has had absences, or an intervention has not happened as often as planned, consider what impact that has had on the effectiveness of the intervention. If the intervention has gone as planned, look at the progress charted and ask yourself these questions:

- Is it swift enough? Is the intervention helping this child to close the gap? Is the adult working with the child the best person for the job?
- Is this the best intervention? Is there anything else you can reasonably do in school?
- What should happen next? If the intervention was successful, do you continue it, develop it, consolidate it or change to a different target?

At the end of the process, create a new RoP with the child and use a new monitoring sheet.

Monitoring the progress of _____ towards meeting

Target _____

Date	Target	Comment	Achieved			

What is dyslexia?

The British Psychological Society (BPS) states that:

> Dyslexia is evident when accurate and fluent word reading and/or spelling develops very incompletely or with great difficulty. This focuses on literacy learning at the 'word level' and implies that the problem is severe and persistent despite appropriate learning opportunities.

(British Psychological Society 1999: reprint 2005, *Dyslexia, Literacy and Psychological Assessment: Report by the Working Party of the Division of Educational and Child Psychology of the British Psychological Society*, BPS, Leicester)

Key aspects of the BPS definition are:

- it focuses on the observable difficulties rather than on any possible 'underlying cause';
- it is not linked to ability;
- the 'severe and persistent' learning difficulty relates to the reading and spelling of individual words rather than text comprehension.

Although the BPS acknowledges that for some children dyslexia is a Specific Learning Difficulty (SpLD), it also recognises that there are other children who have a range of learning difficulties which include dyslexia.

Within the BPS definition, diagnosis of dyslexia does not rely on cognitive skills, but on positive indicators for dyslexia that include difficulties in processing the sounds in speech and linking them to written letters as well as difficulties in short-term or working memory.

In his 2009 Report, *Identifying and Teaching Young People with Dyslexia and Literacy Difficulties*, Sir Jim Rose and his team constructed a six-part working definition of dyslexia:

- Dyslexia is a learning difficulty that primarily affects the skills involved in accurate and fluent word reading and spelling.
- Characteristic features of dyslexia are difficulties in phonological awareness, verbal memory and verbal processing speed.
- Dyslexia occurs across the range of intellectual abilities.
- It is best thought of as a continuum, not a distinct category, and there are no clear cut-off points.
- Co-occurring difficulties may be seen in aspects of language, motor co-ordination, mental calculation, concentration and personal organisation, but these are not, by themselves, markers of dyslexia.

- A good indication of the severity and persistence of dyslexic difficulties can be gained by examining how the individual responds, or has responded, to well-founded intervention.

(Identifying and Teaching Young People with Dyslexia and Literacy Difficulties, Sir Jim Rose et al., 2009, p. 29)

In addition to these characteristics, the British Dyslexia Association acknowledges the visual processing difficulties that some individuals with dyslexia can experience, and points out that dyslexic readers can show a combination of abilities and difficulties that affect the learning process. Some also have strengths in other areas such as design, problem solving, creative skills, interactive skills and oral skills.

Dyslexia is now thought of as a spectrum. Eight per cent or more of the population are affected by dyslexia to some degree, although only about 2–3 per cent of children in school are likely to need specialist intervention. Most children who are experiencing reading difficulties will respond well to small group intervention, but there are a small number of children who are likely to continue to experience persistent and significant difficulties and who will need ongoing individual support.

This 2–3 per cent of children usually find it hard to identify sounds in spoken words, and most have difficulties with short-term memory, sequencing and organisation. This means that it is more difficult for them to learn phonics and to decode (blend to read) and encode (segment to spell) words; they typically need a great deal of instruction. Spelling in particular is not an automatic skill for many dyslexic children; however, most of them learn to read, sometimes very well.

The evidence considered by Sir Jim Rose and his team showed that early, high-quality, focused and personalised intervention could make a significant impact for dyslexic children. But they recommend that dyslexia is seen on a continuum – individuals have different degrees of dyslexia, which become apparent when considering responses to intervention.

The Rose Report presented the following table, which identifies developmental phases of dyslexia in children and young people who are learning to read English:

Developmental phase	Signs of dyslexia	
Preschool	Delayed or problematic speech Poor expressive language	Poor rhyming skills Little interest/difficulty learning letters
Early school years	Poor letter-sound knowledge Poor phoneme awareness Poor word attack skills	Idiosyncratic spelling Problems copying
Middle school years	Slow reading Poor decoding skills when faced with new words Phonetic or non-phonetic spelling	
Adolescence and adulthood	Poor reading fluency Slow speed of writing Poor organisation and expression in work	

Identifying and Teaching Young People with Dyslexia and Literacy Difficulties, Sir Jim Rose et al., 2009, p. 31.

The Rose Report argued that any child who is demonstrating these learning difficulties, in comparison to their typically developing peers, should be given an intervention in school regardless of whether or not any diagnosis of dyslexia has been made.

Dyslexia indicators

The following list is not intended to be used as an assessment tool. Instead it is a list of indicators of dyslexia to facilitate understanding that dyslexia is more complex than confusing 'b' and 'd'. Dyslexia may have implications for a child's performance and attainment across the taught curriculum as well as for behaviour.

Although this is not intended to be used as a screening tool, if you teach a child for whom you would answer *'yes when compared to the majority of children of the same age'* to most of the following questions, it would be wise to seek further advice and, in the interim, to work with the child as if they were dyslexic.

	Yes/No
FAMILY	
Is there anyone in the child's immediate family who is dyslexic?	
SPEECH AND LANGUAGE	
Was the child late to begin talking?	
Was the child slow to pick up new words?	
Is the child's speech sometimes unclear?	
Is the child's speech immature?	
Does the child use a comparatively limited vocabulary?	
PHONOLOGICAL AWARENESS	
Does/did the child take a long time to learn rhymes and nursery rhymes?	
Does the child find it hard to hear whether two words rhyme or to generate rhyming words?	
Does the child find it hard to identify words which begin with the same sound?	
Does the child struggle to orally segment words for spelling (e.g. *mug m-u-g*)?	
Does the child struggle to orally blend words for reading (e.g. *m-u-g mug*)?	
Does/did the child experience difficulties in learning letter-sound relationships?	
Is/was it hard to maintain the child's interest when learning letter-sound relationships?	
Does/did the child take longer to make progress in phonics than the majority of their peers?	
READING	
Does the child sometimes miss a line when reading?	
Does/did the child confuse similar letters and words when reading?	
Is the child over-reliant on pictures?	
Does the child omit words, or add them in?	
Does the child recognise a word on one page, but not on the next?	
Does/did the child track text with their finger after their peers were able to track with eyes only?	
Does the child gain information from pictures, as opposed to the text?	
Does the child read on even if what they have said does not make sense?	

Is the pace of reading slow and hesitant?	
Does the child have particular difficulties when reading longer words?	
Is the child's reading monotonous, with little expression?	
Does the child lose the point of the text and struggle to identify the main idea?	
Is the child's reading attainment much lower than the majority of their peers?	
WRITING AND SPELLING	
Does the child confuse similar letters when writing?	
Does/did the child sometimes do mirror writing (i.e. starting at the right-hand edge of the page)?	
Does/did the child have a poor pencil grip?	
Does the child have relatively poor handwriting?	
Do spelling errors sometimes seem to be 'idiosyncratic'?	
Does the child spell the same word in several different ways in a piece of writing?	
Does the child miss out words when writing?	
Does the child struggle to remember the whole sentence while working out how to spell a word?	
Does the child find it hard to copy quickly and accurately from the board?	
Is the child an unwilling writer?	
Is presentation of written work disappointing?	
Does the child experience difficulty in returning to the margin when beginning a new line of writing?	
Is the child's attainment in writing much lower than the majority of their peers?	
MEMORY AND AUDITORY PROCESSING	
Does the child need a longer than usual 'take-up time' when answering questions?	
Does the child find it hard to repeat or paraphrase what has been said by the teacher?	
Is the child over-reliant on peers in the classroom (e.g. when following instructions)?	
Does the child have difficulty in learning facts in maths and other curriculum areas?	
Is the child forgetful of words and facts?	
Does/did the child struggle to remember sequences (e.g. the alphabet, days of the week)?	
Does/did the child have particular difficulty in understanding concepts of time (e.g. 'yesterday')?	
LEARNING BEHAVIOURS	
Does the child have difficulty in maintaining concentration, especially when reading or writing?	
Does the child appear to find it difficult to pay attention?	
Does the child have difficulty in carrying out a sequence of instructions?	
Does the child give up quickly if they encounter a difficulty?	
Does the child confuse left and right?	
Is the child's recorded work disappointing when compared to their oral work?	
Does the child have curriculum strengths when they are not required to read or write?	
ORGANISATION, CONDUCT AND EMOTIONAL BEHAVIOURS	
Does the child have low self-esteem?	
Does the child engage in 'displacement activities' in order to avoid recorded tasks?	
Does the child sometimes read or write digits in the wrong order?	
Is the child either the 'class clown' or withdrawn?	
Does the child have more difficulty than their peers in getting dressed or tying shoe-laces?	
Is the child disorganised?	

Three questions on this checklist are highlighted in grey. These are the three most important questions: if the answer to all of these is 'yes', and these difficulties are 'severe and persistent' you should start planning a strategy for intervention, whether or not you think the child is dyslexic.

How can I get a diagnosis – and what can I do to help?

> The first step in identifying that children may have language learning difficulties, including dyslexia, is to notice those making poor progress in comparison with their typically developing peers, despite receiving high-quality Wave 1 literacy teaching.
>
> (Adapted from *Identifying and Teaching Young People with Dyslexia and Literacy Difficulties*, Sir Jim Rose et al., 2009, p. 98)

A formal assessment of dyslexia can only be given by an Educational Psychologist or a Specialist Teacher of Dyslexia (contact http://www.dyslexiaaction.org.uk for more information). Some local authorities employ advisory teachers for Specific Learning Difficulties (SpLD) who are specialist teachers; other local authorities are much less willing to formally identify dyslexic children.

For some children – and their parents – a diagnosis is useful because it helps the child to understand why they are having difficulty in reading or spelling; for others, it can become an excuse for making less effort. You know your children. You, your SENCo and the child's parents need to make a decision together about whether or not to pursue a formal diagnosis. Depending on the child's age and performance, a formal assessment for dyslexia is likely to include assessments of: spelling, reading, verbal reasoning, non-verbal reasoning, comprehension, memory, processing speed, phonological awareness, writing speed, organisational skills and approaches to learning.

A formal diagnosis is not necessary to ensure that the child is taught appropriately – a good teacher meets the learning and developmental needs of all the children in the class. All interventions aimed at dyslexic children will benefit any child in the class who is not making appropriate progress in reading and writing.

Although good classroom teaching is the bedrock of all learning, most research suggests that children who are falling behind their peers – particularly in reading and spelling – will benefit from a targeted intervention. Simply doing nothing and hoping that the child will catch up is unlikely to be successful. There is substantial research evidence to show that progress of children with reading and writing difficulties can be improved through successful intervention.

Intervention programmes

There is no one intervention programme that will work with all dyslexic learners: each child is an individual and different programmes will be effective for different children. Key features of successful intervention programmes are likely to include the following:

- multi-sensory approaches, including combinations of visual, auditory and kinaesthetic learning opportunities;

- a systematic, cumulative and repetitive sequence for teaching skills;
- highly structured information, from the simple to the complex;
- regular, short sessions – 'little and often';
- opportunities for reinforcement throughout the day;
- integrated teaching of phonics, spelling, reading and handwriting;
- over-learning, leading to automatic recognition and production, of letter patterns;
- explicit teaching of strategies for reading and writing;
- continuous review and consolidation of previously learned skills;
- careful pacing to avoid information overload;
- explicit teaching to encourage generalisation.

As with all SEN interventions, a successful dyslexia intervention needs to be sensitive to the child's development, pace and learning style. If one approach does not work, you may need to find a different approach. However, all successful programmes will be systematic, structured, cumulative and sequential. The Dyslexia Trust has created a useful interactive tool for identifying appropriate interventions: www.interventionsforliteracy.org.uk

Before you introduce a specific intervention, consider the child's previous experience of being taught to read. For example, has the child experienced daily, systematic phonics teaching? If so, how successful were they? At what point did the teaching stop making an impact? What was the problem identified?

In his 2009 Report, Sir Jim Rose and his team identified key elements of early intervention that make the most impact for any child who is failing to make expected progress in reading:

Phonemic awareness instruction	Teaching children to manipulate the sounds of words (phonemes) to improve reading (blending) and spelling (segmentation) skills.
Phonics instruction	Teaching children how to sound out printed words using knowledge of graphemes, to decode multi-syllabic words, and to generalise learned rules of language to new words.
Spelling and writing instruction	Encouraging children to write letters, sound patterns (graphemes), words, and sentences to support and reinforce segmentation strategies and the acquisition of phonics rules.
Fluency instruction	Providing children with practice in reading words accurately to gain sufficient speed to ensure that comprehension is not impaired because of undue focus on word reading.
Vocabulary instruction	Teaching children to recognise the meaning of words they are reading and to build an appreciation and understanding of new words.
Comprehension instruction	Teaching children to monitor their understanding while reading, linking what they read to previous learning and asking questions about what they read.

(From *Identifying and Teaching Young People with Dyslexia and Literacy Difficulties*, Sir Jim Rose et al., 2009, pp. 64–5)

The earlier an intervention is started, the better the chances the child has of catching up with their peers. Many people feel that dyslexia should not be diagnosed before a child is 7 or 8. However, dyslexic children tend to experience difficulties in learning to read and write well before that age. If group or individual interventions are put in place as soon as a child is seen to be making slower progress than their peers, the impact of dyslexia on that child may be minimised. Many older dyslexic children develop unwelcome classroom behaviours and have poor self-confidence and self-esteem. These factors may partially account for why it is so much harder, although still important, to offer successful interventions at secondary school.

What dyslexic learners find hard

Imagine you are given a brand new, high-specification computer, together with keyboard, mouse, printer and so on and a pile of boxes of exciting-looking software. You put the software in the computer and nothing happens. Eventually you realise that the software is for an entirely different, non-compatible computer. There is nothing wrong with the computer, or with the software: they are just not compatible.

That is a little like being a dyslexic child. Like the computer, the child's brain is probably working perfectly well. Likewise, the content and style of your teaching may be very good – but the two may not be compatible.

Understanding some of the implications for learners can help you to adapt your teaching style to be more inclusive for dyslexia learners. The three interlinked areas which prove problematic to most dyslexic children across the taught curriculum are:

- phonological awareness;
- auditory processing;
- working memory.

Phonological awareness

Think how hard it is to teach a child who says /f/ instead of /th/ to spell words like *thing* or *think* when they are saying and hearing the words /fing/ and /fink/. As far as the child is concerned, *f, ff* and *th* are just alternative way of representing the sound /f/.

Phonological awareness is something that dyslexic children are often weak at. Their 'storage system' for the sounds in English does not necessarily match yours, so they may conflate or confuse sounds. Some sounds in English are more similar than others. Understanding how sounds are made can help you to help the learner to unpick these confusions.

Sounds are articulated in different ways in the mouth, using the tongue and the lips.

Vowels

- **Vowels** are made with an open airstream. The air comes through the mouth and is shaped by the position of the tongue and lips.
- Use mirrors to look at the mouth making vowel sounds: ask children to say /ee/ and /oo/. What changes? Then try moving from /ar/ to /er/ and talk about what you see and what you feel your tongue doing.

Consonants

There are five basic categories of consonant sounds in English, the first three of which can be *voiced* – where the vocal cords vibrate (put your finger and thumb on either side of your voice box and say /zzzzz/ – feel the vibration), or *unvoiced* – where the vocal cords do not vibrate (say /ssss/ and note the voice box does not vibrate).

- **Plosives** are oral consonant sounds in which the airstream is momentarily blocked by the tongue or lips. Plosives can be voiced (for example, /b/ and /g/) or *unvoiced* (for example, /p/ and /k/).
- **Fricatives** are the longer 'hissing' sounds in which the airstream escapes through a nearly closed passage. Fricatives can be voiced or unvoiced (for example, /s/ and /v/).
- **Affricates** are made by a plosive being released into a fricative. Affricates can be voiced or unvoiced (for example, /ch/ and /dg/).
- **Nasals** are sounds in which the airstream is directed down the nose, rather than through the mouth. The sounds are varied by the position of the lips, teeth and tongue. All nasals are voiced (for example, /m/).
- **Liquids and glides** are made when the tongue comes close to another part of the mouth without interrupting the flow of air. Liquids and glides are voiced (for example, /l/ and /r/).

The chart below shows important relationships between the consonant sounds in English.

Where in the mouth the sound is made	Between the lips (bilabial)	Lips and teeth (labio-dental)	Between the teeth (inter-dental)	Behind the teeth (alveolar)	Palate (alveo-palatal)	Back of the mouth (velar)	In the throat (glottal)
Plosive: unvoiced voiced	b p			t d		k g	Glottal stop
Fricative: unvoiced voiced		f v	th (*thin*) th (*this*)	s z	sh zh		h
Affricate: unvoiced voiced					ch dg		
Nasal	m			n		ng	
Glide/liquid	w			r l	y		

Fig. 4: The consonant sounds in English.

Understanding these relationships helps us to understand how easy it is to confuse certain sounds, particularly for children whose hearing is uncertain, for example, due to colds and glue ear. To a child who is relying to some extent on lip-reading /m/, /p/ and /b/ all look the same.

Teach children to explore the full range of sounds, using mirrors so that they can see how their mouth moves to shape the sounds they are making, and encouraging them to talk about how their tongue is touching the inside of their mouth.

If a child is not able to imitate any of the sounds, you will need to seek advice from a speech and language therapist.

Auditory processing difficulties

'Auditory processing' is the medical term for 'listening'. It is thought that up to about 10 per cent of children have perfectly good hearing, but their ability to listen, understand and retain what they have heard may be impaired. This is an auditory processing difficulty or disorder (APD).

Children who have APD typically have difficulty with:

- understanding, no matter how hard they try;
- separating the target sound (for example, the teacher's voice) from background sounds;
- expressing themselves clearly;
- reading and understanding;
- remembering and following instructions;
- remembering sequences and sequencing sounds;
- recognising rhythm and patterns in sound;
- staying focused, paying attention and concentrating;
- processing spoken language at speed.

Children with APD experience particular difficulties in phonics, especially when it comes to distinguishing between similar sounds, at speed. So distinguishing between words like *list* and *lift* or *do* and *to* is problematical. Saying and remembering the sequence of sounds in a word is very often challenging, so a child may sound out /c-l-ow-n/ and say *now*, because they only remember the last two sounds they said and heard. Although learning phonics presents greater than usual difficulties for children with APD, it is still a crucial skill for them to learn. As soon as possible, however, children with APD will benefit from being taught to 'chunk' words into, for example, recognised parts of words, syllables, base words + suffixes. This will reduce the sequencing load on the memory.

One significant implication of not hearing sounds or rhythms precisely is that it is very easy for a child with APD to entirely misinterpret what has been said. By mishearing a few sounds, and breaking up the streams of words in the wrong places, children can 'hear' a completely different message from the one you think you said. Some adult sufferers compare it to having a bad reception over the phone: you hear bits of speech and have to fill in the gaps by making assumptions.

The area which is most distressing for children with APD is often during whole-class teaching time. Children with APD find it especially difficult to work when the environment is noisy, because they are not able to filter out distracting sounds and decide what to focus on. The children also need additional 'take-up time' when being asked a question. They can find this distressing because while they are desperately trying to remember what you said and retrieving the answer, other children are waving their hands in the air, sighing deeply or just shouting out the answer. Not only are these behaviours distracting to the child with APD, but the child starts to feel as if they are 'stupid'. Teachers often unintentionally reinforce this opinion by asking another child to give the answer if the child with APD is taking too long. Advice is that teachers should typically allow up to 10 seconds 'take-up time' when asking questions in class. For a child with APD, this may need to be stretched to as much as 30 seconds.

Many children with APD are referred back to the audiologist time after time because parents and teachers believe that the children cannot hear. However, even children whose hearing is perfectly normal often begin to use clues which are more typically associated with people with more profound hearing impairments. For example, children with APD often lip-read to try to 'fill in the blanks', so the children should be seated near the front of the class where they can see your whole face.

Key classroom strategies when supporting a child who may have APD include the following:

- Always say their name to gain their attention before speaking to them.
- Minimise other distractions while you are talking.
- Simplify instructions.
- Use visuals to support instructions and information shared.
- Ask the child to tell you what they have to do or what they have learned as soon as possible at the end of a session.
- Pre-teach critical vocabulary and ideas.
- Teach the child to 'home in' on key words (generally nouns, verbs and descriptors) instead of trying to process all of the information in a sentence.
- If the child can read, write instructions and summaries for the child to keep and refer to later.

Working memory

Working memory is the system which allows us to hold information in our heads while we do tasks such as reasoning and comprehension. Classroom activities involving working memory include, for example: following a sequence of instructions; adding three numbers; reading and saying the sounds of a word prior to blending them; remembering a sentence while we focus on spelling a word; following a conversation or a taught session; contributing to a class discussion; copying text; reading comprehension activities.

Most dyslexic children have poor working memories. A 2008 study by Gathercole and Alloway identified that pupils whose working memory is in the bottom 10 per cent of the population exhibit the following characteristics:

- normal social relationships with peers;
- being reserved in group activities;
- poor academic progress in reading and maths;
- difficulties in following instructions;
- problems with learning activities that require both storage and processing;
- place-keeping difficulties;
- appearing to be inattentive, to have a short attention span, and to be distractible.

(Susan Gathercole and Tracy Packiam Alloway, *Working Memory and Learning: A Practical Guide for Teachers*. SAGE Publications, 2008)

The major difference between a child with poor working memory and one with Attention Deficit Hyperactivity Disorder (ADHD) is that the behaviour of children with poor working memory is fairly consistent, whereas that of ADHD children tends to fluctuate from time to time or day to day. Many children with ADHD also have poor working memories.

Gathercole and Alloway suggest that the reason why these children make poor academic progress is because they are unable to meet the memory demands of structured learning activities. Their working memory quickly becomes overloaded and they forget key information they need to successfully complete the task. They either need to be reminded, or they will guess, or copy someone else, or abandon the task – and often disguise it with off-task behaviours. Every time this happens, the child loses a learning opportunity and these lost opportunities tend to be cumulative and result in delayed learning.

Here are some suggestions for overcoming these memory difficulties in the classroom:

- Every 5 minutes or so, pause and ask children to share ideas with a talk partner. These can include summarising for each other, asking each other questions, or trying to agree on the most important point you made.
- Use visuals as much as possible to accompany teaching. Leave them on display in the sequence in which you introduced them.
- Expect to re-visit key ideas with some of the children. Have individual copies of visuals as a guide.
- Teach children to use mind maps and other visual organisers to record in words or sketches while you are talking.
- Allow children to make audio recordings of what they plan to write so they don't forget.
- Teach children to plan for writing and other tasks.
- Use a range of guided listening techniques to keep the children alert while you are talking.
- Teach children approved strategies in your classroom for finding out what they have forgotten. If they think you are going to be cross or disappointed with them, they will be reluctant to try to find out what they should know.

Supporting children with poor phonological awareness, APD and/or working memory

Although there are assessments available for each of these individual difficulties, most dyslexic children will have all of them to a greater or lesser extent. Organising your classroom and your teaching to accommodate all of the difficulties is sensible, particularly since strategies for addressing one will generally also help with all the others. Teaching children with these difficulties how to be successful in your classroom will give them invaluable life skills as well as increasing the likelihood of their learning.

The dyslexia-friendly classroom

A dyslexia-friendly classroom is a learner-friendly classroom, since all learners will benefit from strategies put in place to support those with dyslexia. The following checklist is divided into sections containing suggestions for particular parts of the curriculum and the school day. Different suggestions will be appropriate for different age groups and children. Some of the ideas will be appropriate for your situation, whereas there will be good reasons why others are less suitable for you. You should take from this list only what is relevant for the learners in your classroom and for you.

General advice
- Offer structured, small-steps teaching with over-learning built in.
- Make learning active, with positive feedback and focused praise.
- Show, don't just tell. Make maximum use of ICT.
- Create a multi-sensory teaching environment. Use images, diagrams, flowcharts, colours, mind maps, sounds, tactile objects ...
- Include active, problem-solving approaches.
- Seat dyslexic children close to you so that you can check discreetly if they have understood and you can pick up on non-verbal communication if they are struggling.
- Reduce copying from books, worksheets or the board. If there must be copying from the board, use different coloured dots for different lines or number the lines. Provide worksheets and photocopies of work (for example, sentences to be completed) or lists of instructions for homework.
- Clearly mark resources, and display a visual timetable.
- Give clear indicators of time left.
- Give time to finish pleasurable tasks at a later point.
- Be patient and be prepared to repeat yourself several times.
- As far as possible, ensure that the classroom is peaceful and free from distractions.
- Allow full access to the subjects dyslexic children are good at.

Giving instructions
- Keep instructions short and issue them one at a time.
- Provide visual support where plausible.
- Break down longer instructions into smaller chunks.
- Use consistent language when giving instructions.

Whole-class teaching sessions

- Organise a teaching assistant to pre-teach key vocabulary and concepts. Flashcards can be a useful follow-up during the lesson itself.
- Always give the big picture – an overview of a lesson – at the beginning, and a summary at the end.
- Make expectations very clear.
- Explain → check for understanding → expect to repeat with pictures.
- Display the topic, key words, date and day on the whiteboard.
- Repeat key words and phrases.
- Allow for individual thinking time or discussion with a partner before bringing the subject back to the whole class.
- Have high, but attainable, and consistent expectations.
- Be enthusiastic and keep to the point.
- Encourage children to ask questions.
- Provide opportunities for children to show creative thinking and learning and be prepared to recognise and reward creativity in approaches and solutions to problems as well as through drama, music and so on.
- Provide subject glossaries in hard copy and electronic format.
- Use 'pay attention now' words such as *listen carefully*.

Planning and organisation (for older children)

- Give children colour-coded timetables, where the colour coding aids organisation skills.
- Teach examples of planning strategies, for example, concept maps, flowcharts, timelines.
- Give written homework instructions.
- Pair children with homework buddies to allow parents to check homework.

Listening

- Slow down your speech and make sentence structures simple.
- Teach guided listening strategies.
- Teach children how to use visualisation and make pictures in their heads. Pictures are more easily remembered than lots of auditory words.
- Take pauses to give children thinking time.
- Allow time for processing – children may need extra time to think through what has been said.
- Vary the pitch, tone and speed of your delivery to keep the children engaged.
- Check that the child has understood, by asking them to retell what they have to do (not in public). Children should not be allowed to become dependent on their friends for information.

Phonics and spelling

- Teach systematically – little and often.
- Provide opportunities to practise what has been taught throughout the school day.
- Create an expectation that what has been learned will be used.

- Display groups of graphemes where children can see them easily.
- Display cue cards for specific spelling rules or difficulties with reversals etc.
- Use displays to support key graphemes/vocabulary and reinforce daily.
- Give cue card key rings to support spelling.
- Provide written spelling lists for homework practice – don't expect children to copy them down.
- Provide appropriate dictionaries/thesauruses – electronic ones may be best.

Writing

- Provide suitable writing tools, including ICT (for example, digital recorder, laptop).
- Give a choice of handwriting tools and pencil grips.
- Encourage different ways of recording information.
- Teach strategies to help with planning written work.
- Mark separately for content and for spelling and punctuation.
- If there are a lot of mis-spellings, only mark high-frequency words and compile a personal checklist of the words.
- Teach children different ways of recording thoughts and outcomes.
- Encourage children to speak or record their thoughts before writing them.

Reading

- Provide books appropriate to the child's age as well as their reading stage.
- Do not ask children to read aloud unless they want to. Reading silently may work better.
- Encourage paired reading and reading with parents as well as reading in school.
- Encourage children to listen to audio books.
- Read e-books online together.

Comprehension

- Encourage children to use a highlighter pen for key words/concepts.
- Highlight and discuss new subject vocabulary.
- Use visual cues to support reading.
- Check understanding through discussion, asking the child to present the information in a different way, using role-play and so on.
- Teach the SQ3R approach (skim reading, skim questions, read, recite, review).
- Teach the use of key words and phrases such as *who*, *what*, *where*, *when*, *why*, and *how much*, *therefore*, *in addition*, *consequently*, *next*, *finally*, *in conclusion*, and so on.

Visual

- Change the background colour on interactive whiteboards: black on white can cause strain for some children.
- Use cream paper, not white paper, for children who have visual stress.
- Avoid too much print on any side of paper. Aim for minimum 12 point type and 1.5 line spacing. Include images.

Maths

- Teach children how to use support materials.
- Recognise that an extended use of concrete materials may be required.
- Put number work into practical contexts.
- Small packs of cards may be provided to aid the repetition and over-learning of number bonds, tables and so on. Write the question on one side and the answer on the other. The child can then work through the pack from either side.
- Pelmanism and other matching games will help with reinforcement.
- Display an analogue and digital clock side by side for reinforcement. The digital clock is easier to read but does not help the child understand time.

Self-esteem

- Allow access to a variety of ways of recording and presenting knowledge.
- Recognise and reinforce strengths.
- Carefully differentiate learning tasks without over-reliance on worksheets.
- Group children according to their levels of understanding and interest in the topics, not according to literacy abilities.
- Praise work for effort and content and not only accuracy.
- Consider seating arrangements and promote peer support.
- Give clear recognition that the child is intelligent, even if they can't always record responses.

Access to resources

- Have an alphabet strip on each desk and a number square on each table to cut down on memory work.
- Give children immediate and easy access to resources.
- Use writing mats showing high-frequency and topic words, and also known graphemes in groups.

Questions

Encourage children to apply the following questions to all of their work:

Purpose	Why am I doing this? 'Do I know what the objectives are for this lesson?'
Outcome	What is the required end product? 'Do I know what a good example of this would look like?'
Strategy	What strategy should be used? 'Do I know which strategies I can use to help me achieve this?'
Monitoring	Was it successful? 'Did I meet the learning objective for this lesson?'
Development	How can it be improved? 'Could I have done it better?'
Transfer	Can it be transferred to another skill? 'What have I learned from this lesson that I could use in another subject or situation?'

(From *Identifying and Teaching Young People with Dyslexia and Literacy Difficulties*, Sir Jim Rose et al., 2009, p. 124)

Dyslexia and numeracy

Although dyslexia is primarily a difficulty with words (from the Greek *dys* = difficult and *lexis* = word), it has implications for maths too. There are a lot of similarities between literacy and numeracy, including the following:

- Both are taught using words – so a child who experiences difficulty with words is likely to experience difficulties with other curriculum areas.
- Both are based on sequences of abstract shapes – and children with dyslexia tend to struggle to learn and to read sequences.
- Both assume good short-term memory – and this is a known difficulty for dyslexic children.

About 60 per cent of dyslexic children experience difficulties with maths – although for many of these youngsters, their maths is still stronger than their literacy. However, about 11 per cent of dyslexic children excel in maths and the remaining 29 per cent do as well as their peers. (These statistics come from the British Dyslexia Association's *Dyslexia-Friendly Schools* pack.)

Teaching styles

It should be presupposed that dyslexic children will be weak at maths and it will be important that their teacher looks for approaches which are successful with dyslexic children. All of the 'dyslexia-friendly' approaches on pages 34–7 are equally applicable for maths teaching. In particular, dyslexic children will benefit from the following:

- Multi-sensory teaching.
- Continued access to concrete aids – probably for long after their peers.
- Opportunities to record mental strategies, since 'holding a number in their heads' may be challenging.
- Being explicitly taught a range of strategies and encouraged to find those that 'work'.
- Games. There are many maths games available – and many that can be played on a computer, downloaded or made at school – which enable all children to consolidate their learning in a motivating and comparatively stress-free way.

Numeracy difficulties

Some particular difficulties for dyslexic children	Some ways of helping
Understanding the language of maths, particularly in problem solving (e.g. different words which mean 'add' or 'subtract') and the fact that the same word can have different meanings in different contexts.	• Encourage children to make their own lists of words that can share a meaning in particular contexts. • Allow children to use maths mats with lists of key words. • Pre-teach vocabulary in context before the lesson. • Focus teaching on estimation, in order that children can check the likelihood of their answers.
Understanding how operations relate to each other (e.g. subtraction by counting on may seem counterintuitive).	• Create continuing opportunities to consolidate learning with concrete apparatus. • Teach children to 'problematise' number sentences (e.g. *I have 43 eggs and I use 17 of them for breakfast. How many eggs do I have left?*) and use apparatus to find the answer. • Encourage the use of calculators – combined with estimation.
Recalling and using times tables and number bonds.	• Teach understanding using concrete and real life examples (e.g. sharing biscuits between friends; counting pairs of socks; and so on). • Teach times tables to music. • Teach children how to use what they know to work out what they don't know.
Adding or subtracting columns of numbers.	• Teach children to break the column down into a number of smaller operations.
Knowing the order in which to perform an operation (e.g. 'take 32 from 53' – which number do you take from which?).	• Lay out addition and subtraction sentences on triangles, emphasising that the biggest number must always be at the top. Teach children how to work out the four number sentences that can be derived from a number triangle (e.g. $5 + 7 = 12$; $7 + 5 = 12$; $12 - 7 = 5$; $12 - 5 = 7$). Once they understand the logic of the triangle, the numbers become easier to work with.
Memorising sequences in order to complete an operation (e.g. when doing column subtraction, what has to be done first?).	• Allow practice with plenty of time. • Break the sequence down into steps and practise the steps one at a time. • Allow the children to sequence examples that have previously been worked out. • Encourage the child to 'talk it through', using their own logic to explain why one step has to precede another.
Working at speed to solve mental maths problems.	• Teach the child how to do jottings during mental maths sessions. • Ask the child to tell you what they need to know by heart – then help them to learn those number facts. • Practise!
Understanding place value.	• Use concrete apparatus – many children find £1, 10p and 1p coins easier to relate to than specific place value resources. • Use place value cards to emphasise the order of digits – and particularly 0.
Copying sums and longer digits accurately, both when copying from a book and when transferring numbers while doing a sum.	• Use colour. • Teach children to say numbers out loud as they read and write them.

The Target Ladders

Aspect 1: Phonological awareness

Letter	Rhyming activities	Generating rhymes	Hearing sounds/alliteration	Identifying syllables	P scale/ NC level
A	Listens to rhymes		Breaks the flow of speech into words – can say how many words have been spoken		P4
A	Responds to rhymes	Understands vocabulary: *beginning, end, same*	Repeats a word or non-word	Moves rhythmically to music	
B	Joins in with actions			Shows an awareness of rhythm in music activities	
B		Generates a string of rhyming syllables	Repeats a given 'long' sound (e.g. /w/, /a/, /s/)	Repeats a three-syllable word that an adult has said	
C	Joins in with the refrain or 'interesting' part of the rhyme	Completes the rime in a rhyming pair (e.g. man, c_ _?)	Repeats a given 'short' sound (e.g. /p/, /t/, /g/)	Joins in with a simple, repeated clapping rhythm	P5
C	Joins in with some rhyming words in the number rhyme	Begins to recognise the word *rhyme*		Copies simple rhythms	
D	Will complete a familiar number rhyme if started		Can say if two sounds are the same	Tries to join in when an adult says a name, clapping the syllables	P6
D	Can say the missing rhyming word in a familiar nursery rhyme	Can say whether or not two words rhyme	Identifies the dominant sound in a tongue-twister	Claps the syllables in a two- or three-syllable word	

40   *The Target Ladders*

Suggested activities

Vocabulary check

This vocabulary is important because we use it when we talk about phonological awareness.

- Arrange three different plastic animals standing in a queue for a feeding trough. Can children tell you which animal:
  - is at the *beginning* of the queue?
  - is at the *start* of the queue?
  - does the queue *begin* with?
  - does the queue *start* with?
  - is at the *end* of the queue?
  - does the queue *end* with?
  - is in the *middle* of the queue?
- Repeat the activity using concrete examples, for example:
  - Make a queue of children at the classroom door.
  - Use small world people to form a queue at a bus stop.

Playing with rhyme

Make your classroom a place which is rich in language play and rhyming.

- Teach age-appropriate rhymes – nursery rhymes, number rhymes, action rhymes, songs, silly poems. Create an expectation that children will participate in them when you re-read them, sing them or say them again.
- Take every opportunity to respond to a situation with a rhyme. Make up classroom rhymes, stressing the rhyming words (for example, *When you've finished playing in the sand, sweep it up then wash your hands.*) They don't have to be great poetry!
- Encourage playing with language, making rhyming strings. Model the activity yourself.
- Dismiss children for playtime by saying rhymes of the children's names.
- Make up silly rhyming couplets and ask children to fill in the missing word.

Tongue-twisters

Make your classroom a place which is rich in language play and tongue-twisters. (For this purpose, 'tongue-twisters' simply refers to a phrase or sentence which has lots of words featuring the same sound.) Use sounds which the children can mimic and articulate clearly.

- Focus on 'long' consonant sounds first (for example, /s/, /m/, /n/, /l/) because these are easiest to emphasise in a word.
- Show a variety of objects which begin with the same sound and make up silly sentences (for example, *The snake saw the sausages sizzling in the sun. The long lion lay on the lounger licking a lemon lolly.*) Can children hear the main sound in each sentence?
- When you say your tongue-twister, ask children to do an action (for example, ring a bell, put their hands up, jump on the spot) whenever they hear the target sound.
- When you ask children to repeat sounds, let them first watch you making the sound, then let them look at themselves making the sound in a mirror. Linking the sound to a visual and a movement will help them to identify it more clearly.

Copy me

Play simple games with the children in which they copy your movements. For example:

- Clap your hands twice, then tap your knees twice. Repeat. Encourage children to feel the rhythm and the pattern.
- Walk on the spot, then run. Clap your hands to match your movements. Can children tell what changes? Can they copy you?
- Try changing from a walking clap to a skipping clap. Can children join in and change from one to the other too?

Aspect 1: Phonological awareness

Letter	Rhyming activities	Generating rhymes	Hearing sounds/alliteration	Identifying syllables	P scale/ NC level
E	Recites a familiar nonsense rhyme independently		Points to an object 'beginning with' a sound	Segments a word and says the syllables (e.g. *cro-co-dile*)	P7
E	Completes a variation of a known rhyme by selecting from a choice of three words	Can say a word that rhymes with a given monosyllabic word	Says the sound at the beginning of a word	Claps the syllables in their own name while saying the name aloud	
F		Lists at least two words or non-words to rhyme with a given monosyllabic word	Identifies the final sound in a word	Listens to an adult clapping the syllables and chooses the right animal from a set of three	P8
F	Completes a variation of a known rhyme by generating an appropriate rhyming word			Blends two or three syllables and identifies the word (e.g. what is *mac-a-ro-ni?*)	
G	Recites a variety of rhymes and songs	Lists at least three words or non-words to rhyme with a given monosyllabic word	Blends three heard sounds to make a word (e.g. adult says *c-a-t*)	Joins in clapping the rhythm of known songs and rhymes	1
G	Identifies two objects that rhyme out of a set of three		Identifies two objects that begin with the same sound out of a set of three	Says the second syllable only of a word when an adult has said the first syllable (e.g. *don-key*)	
H	Sings the alphabet using rhyme and rhythm as reminders	Lists a range of words or non-words to rhyme with a given monosyllabic word	Segments sounds in a CVC word (e.g. *d-o-g; sh-ee-p*)	Uses the word 'syllable'	1
H	Identifies the rhyming odd-one-out in a set of three objects			Says the number of syllables in a word or phrase	

42   *The Target Ladders*

© *Target Ladders: Dyslexia*   LDA   Permission to Photocopy

Suggested activities

Reciting rhymes

Teach the children to recite simple rhymes with actions. The language from the rhymes will enrich their writing. Older children will respond well to silly rhymes and raps.

- Provide visual cues to help with sequencing the words and actions.
- Ask children to pair up so one does the action while the other recites the words.
- Prepare for a performance either in assembly or to parents.

Changing rhymes

Collect pictures or small world objects and display them in front of you to give children hints about words they might use as you change the rhymes, for example:

Humpty Dumpty sat on a box
Humpty Dumpty saw a _____
Humpty Dumpty sat on a chair
Humpty Dumpty saw a _____
Humpty Dumpty sat on a log
Humpty Dumpty saw a _____
and so on.

Generating rhymes

Many dyslexic children find it hard to generate rhymes. To help them, make sets of pictures and objects in order to give visual cues.

- Initially, when you ask a child to *'Tell me something that rhymes with clock'*, have three or four pictures on show – as well as the picture of the clock. If necessary, move the picture of the clock beside each of the pictures and say (for example) clock-tree, clock-fish, clock-sock, clock-wall. Which of these sound the same at the end of the word?
- Once children can do this, start modelling how you can produce whole strings of rhyming words and non-words, for example, *clock, sock, tock, zock, lock, bock, hock* ...

Follow a similar procedure when identifying words that begin with the same sound.

Eye-Spy

When children are ready to identify sounds at the beginning of words, introduce the activity gradually and spend time consolidating it. It is an important and fundamental skill, so don't rush it.

- Begin with two or three objects on a table. Make sure that the objects are familiar and that the words have very different sounds in them (for example, *hat, pin; book, top; mug, pen; scissors, car*).
- Begin the session by asking the children to name the things on the table.
- Ask them to point to the thing that 'begins with the sound ...'

It does not matter if the words have tricky spellings – you are only trying to hear the first sound. Initially, try to avoid words beginning with adjacent consonants (crocodile, spider, train) because they alter the children's perception of the first sound.

Once children can reliably do this, vary the vocabulary you use:

○ *Begins with the sound ...*
○ *Starts with the sound ...*
○ *Beginning with ...*
○ *Starting with ...*

Gradually increase the number of objects you use, and the similarity between the sounds.

Aspect 1: Phonological awareness

Aspect 1: Phonological awareness

Letter	Rhyming activities	Generating rhymes	Hearing sounds/alliteration	Identifying syllables	NC level
I		Groups words that go together because they rhyme		Deletes syllables in compound words (e.g. says *lighthouse* without the *light*)	1
I			Blends four heard sounds to make a word (e.g. adult says *t-r-ai-n*)	Deletes syllables in non-compound words (e.g. says *banana* without the *na*)	
J	Uses rime and rhymes to remember curriculum facts	Suggests rhymes for words with more than one syllable	Looks at a picture of a CVCC or CCVC word and says the sounds		2
J			Says a word without the first phoneme (e.g. *cat–c → at*)	Replaces final syllables (e.g. says *dinosaur* with *see* instead of *saur*)	
K			Replaces the first sound in a word (e.g. *cat* with an *m → mat*)		2
K			Says a word without the final phoneme (e.g. *cat–t → ca*)	Replaces first syllables (e.g. says *dinosaur* with *gab* instead of *din*: *gabosaur*)	
L			Replaces the final sound in a word (e.g. *cat* with a *p → cap*)		2
L			Says a word without an adjacent consonant (*trap–r → tap*)		

44 *The Target Ladders*

© *Target Ladders: Dyslexia* LDA Permission to Photocopy

Suggested activities

Curriculum rhymes

Use rhyme to help children to remember curriculum facts. There are well-known rhymes such as:

- Months:
  Thirty days have September,
  April, June, and November;
  All the rest have thirty-one,
  Excepting February alone,
  Which has but twenty-eight days clear,
  And twenty-nine on each leap year.

But you can also invent rhymes with movement to teach particular concepts to your class, for example:

- Rounding. If a number ends with ...
  One two three four, take it back to the ten before.
  Five, six, seven, eight, nine, take it to the next in line.

These rhymes do not need to be good poetry – they just need to be good enough to support a poor memory.

Blending and segmenting

- Use 'phonic fingers' when segmenting and blending.
  - *For blending*: Hold up one finger on your left hand as you say each sound in a word (for example, *s-l-ee-p* = 4 sounds = 4 fingers). As you hold up each finger and say the sound, point at that finger with the forefinger of your right hand. When you have said all of the sounds, pull the finger of your left hand across the fingers of your left hand and say the whole word (for example, *s-l-ee-p*, *sleep*).
  - *For segmenting*: say the word first. Then use phonic fingers as for blending.
- 'Stretch' the word to aid blending and segmenting. Whispering the word (for example, *ssss-lll-eeeee-p*) often helps.
- When teaching blending, begin with two or three visuals (either objects or pictures) so that children have a limited number of words to focus on.

Phoneme deletion and replacement

This skill is not as irrelevant as it sounds. In order to read and write efficiently, children need to be able to hold and analyse information in their heads. Try asking them to do the following:

- Say a word and tell you which sound comes after ... (for example, say *sheep*. Which sound comes after /ee/?).
- Spell a simple word, then spell it again with a different letter in a defined place. (For example, spell *cap*. Now spell it again with an /l/ after the /c/. Which word have you made?)

Activities like this are easily developed into useful strategies for spelling. If children can be taught to think about known words and amend them, they will find spelling much easier to conquer.

Splitting compound words

This is a good activity for spelling because it breaks down the information overload and a good activity for reading because it helps children to recognise letter patterns at syllable and word boundaries.

- Begin by asking children to read simple compound words (for example, *bedroom*). Ask them to show you where the word boundary is and to explain how they know.
- Ask them to cover over part of the word and tell you just the other part.
- Repeat the activity orally. Can the child orally split the word into two?
- Make the compound words longer (*jellyfish*, *mountaintop*). Can children still complete the activity both in writing and orally?

Aspect 1: Phonological awareness

45

Aspect 1: Phonological awareness

Letters	Rhyming activities	Generating rhymes	Hearing sounds/alliteration	Identifying syllables	NC level
M			Can explain how you would have to change a word, for example, to make *tap* into *tape*	Replaces middle syllables (e.g. says *dinosaur* with *yes* instead of *no*)	3
M			Can swap round the first sounds of two words (e.g. *happy child, chappy hild*)		

Suggested activities

Note: As children's phonological awareness develops, they are developing skills to become better spellers and readers.

Changing a word

Ask children to work in threes.

- Player 1 says a word. Player 2 says a spelling-related word. Player 3 explains how the words are different (for example, [1] *clap*, [2] *claps* [3] *you added an 's'*.)
- Players take it in turn to be [1], [2] and [3].
- Player 2 earns a point if they say a proper word; Player 3 earns a point if they explain the difference.
- Players 2 and 3 can challenge Player 1 if they think that Player 1 has used a word that cannot be changed within the rules of the game. If they have a successful challenge, they gain a point; otherwise, Player 1 gains a point.
- Once children are familiar with the game, vary the rules:
  - Player 2 has to take something away from the word.
  - Player 2 has to add something between the first and last letters
  - Player 2 has to change a letter rather than taking anything away.
- Throughout the game, ask one of the children to scribe so that the words are recorded for later discussion and spelling.

Syllable boundaries

Ask children to close their eyes and type for 30 seconds as fast as they can. They should not put in any spaces and do not need to worry about making words.

- In pairs, ask children to review what they have typed and see if they can spot any plausible syllables. They should highlight their 'syllables'.
- Talk about how they recognise syllables:
  - There must be one vowel sound and only one vowel sound (although of course the sound can be represented by more than one letter).
  - The vowel sound is likely to be supported by consonants on at least one side of it.
  - The consonant strings must be plausible in English.
- Once children have identified their syllables, ask them to read the syllables. Can they join more than one of their syllables together to make a two- or three-syllable word for others to read?

Aspect 2: Visual and auditory perception and memory

Letters	Visual perception	Visual memory	Auditory perception	Auditory memory	P scale/ NC level
A	Completes six-piece jigsaw independently	Matches symbols and photographs to objects	Matches audio of common animal sounds to pictures of the animals	Responds appropriately to simple closed question	
A	Sorts by colour, size and shape	Draws a person with a head, limbs, eyes and mouth	Recognises the melody to familiar songs	Responds to an instruction with two information-carrying words	
B	Sorts objects in various shades of one colour from darkest to lightest	Looks at a simple shape, then draws it from memory	Tries to clap along to the beat of a familiar tune or song	Joins in with repeated refrains	P6
B	Matches letters and short words	Draws a person with a head, body, limbs, eyes, nose and mouth	Hears a target sound or word against a noisy background	Follows two simple instructions in order (e.g. *Pick up the pencil and sit down*)	
C	Recognises own name	Remembers a detail from a simple picture to answer a question	Identifies common environmental sounds and says whether they are: soft/loud; near/far	Remembers a sequence of three numbers or things	P7
C	Arranges things in order from smallest to largest	Reproduces correct shape for some letters and numbers	Repeats a given sound	Repeats a sentence with up to 12 syllables	
D	Groups objects that vary in two parameters (e.g. red square, red circle, red triangle)	Remembers a detail from a simple picture and reproduces it	Identifies whether two similar sounds are the same (e.g. /t/, /k/; /s/, /sh/)	Predicts the end of an unfinished short story	P8
D	Distinguishes similar shapes (e.g. rectangle/square; circle/oval; triangle/diamond)	Remembers, and reproduces from memory, a sequence of three images	Articulates age-appropriate sounds correctly	Carries a simple message to a familiar classroom	

The Target Ladders

© *Target Ladders: Dyslexia*   LDA   Permission to Photocopy

Suggested activities

Parts and wholes

Some children have difficulty recognising the relationship between an object or symbol in its entirety and the component parts which make it up. So, for example, a child may recognise a word without being able to identify any of its letters; or be able to see a familiar string of letters without recognising the word.

- Use masking tools on interactive whiteboards so that children only see part of a picture. Gradually increase what they can see. How soon can they see the whole thing?
- Cut a simple picture into ten pieces. Present them one at a time. How soon can children tell you what they are looking at?
- In black and white, photocopy words made from magnetic letters. Time children as they make the same words using the magnetic letters (they can put the letters over the photocopy, or line them up underneath).
- On squared paper, draw the 'shapes' of common words with boxes reading up for ascenders and down for descenders; represent 'long' letters (for example, *m, w*) with two boxes. Can children fit the words into their shapes?

Visual memory games

Memory games with simple pictures are readily available, but you can easily and cheaply make your own versions, which meet the precise learning and contextual needs of your children.

- Make your own games using pictures that relate to a curriculum topic you are studying.
- Download free images from the internet which show different examples of the same thing (for example, two different cats or cars). In the memory game, ask the children to match the two different pictures.
- Use a digital camera to take snaps of objects from a different point of view. In the memory game, ask children to match these slightly different pictures.

Play versions of Kim's game.

- Arrange two or three objects on a tray. Let children look at them for 5 seconds. Cover the tray.
  - Ask children to say what was on the tray.
  - Quickly remove or replace one of the items. Uncover the tray. Can the children tell you what has changed?
  - Quickly swap the positions of two items. Uncover the tray. Can the children tell you what has changed?
- As children improve at the game, increase the number of items on the tray.

Auditory perception games

Lotto games featuring CDs of animal and environmental noises are readily available. You can make your own version for your children.

- Use the video on a mobile phone or use a video camera as you walk round school. When you hear a noise which is specific to its location (for example, staffroom kettle boiling; sound of feet running in the hall; computers waking up in the computer suite) take a video – with audio – of what is making the noise.
- Play a sample noise from your walk. Can children identify what they are hearing and remember where they heard it? If they are right, replay the video for them.

Do as I say, not as I do

Teach the children to play 'Simon Says'. Extend the game to include sequences of two or more actions.

Put the children in threes. Each child can take it in turns to be Simon. At any time, one child is Simon, one has to do as Simon says and the third is the monitor who needs to check whether the rules are followed. Give each child three consecutive turns in their role so they understand it. Sample all of the monitors as they carry out their role: do they all know what is expected of them? Can they say whether or not the instruction has been given and followed correctly?

Aspect 2: Visual and auditory perception and memory

Letters	Visual perception	Visual memory	Auditory perception	Auditory memory	P scale/ NC level
E	Identifies most lower case letters	Plays Kim's game with three objects	Identifies whether two words are the same or different (e.g. *dog, dug; pan, pan*)	Recognises if two sentences are given in a sensible order or not (e.g. *Put on your shoes. Put on your socks.*)	P8
E	Matches letters in a group of similar letters (e.g. '*p*'s in a group of '*b*'s; '*a*'s in a group of '*o*'s)	Recognises first 30 tricky words	Identifies pictures for 'minimal pairs' where words begin with different sounds (e.g. *deer/gear; bear/tear*)	Puts hand up to answer a simple question – and gives appropriate response	
F	Reads all the sounds in a CVC word in order and blends them to say the word	Remembers details from a picture to answer three questions	Repeats an unfamiliar three-syllable word	Adds another member to a set of things given orally (e.g. *rabbit, mouse, hamster* …?)	1
F	Counts up to five objects moving eyes only	Reproduces from memory a sequence of three abstract symbols	Joins in clapping the rhythm of known songs and rhymes	Remembers three characters/events/items in a medium-length story	
G	Follows print with eyes only, except when working out a difficult word	Recognises familiar words in a variety of contexts	Blends three heard sounds and says a word	Completes a simple activity without prompting or seeking help	
G	Classifies things: explains why things belong in one set rather than in another	Identifies a word seen for 10 seconds, then hidden, from a choice of two words	Continues a string of rhyming words	Suggests solution to simple problems or riddles presented orally	1
H	Finds five differences in detail between two similar pictures	Reproduces from memory a sequence of four letters, numbers or symbols	Identifies the 'silly word' in a sentence (e.g. *I built a drink of milk*)	Remembers number bonds of 10	
H	Completes a drawing or letter when only part is presented	Recognises 100 high-frequency words	Blends three heard syllables and says a word	Recites alphabet by heart	

Suggested activities

Scotopic sensitivity/Irlen Syndrome

- Indications that Scotopic sensitivity may be a problem include:
  - mis-reading words;
  - skipping lines or words;
  - confusing letters or words that look similar;
  - showing poor comprehension or needing to re-read to get information;
  - losing the place on the page, particularly across line breaks;
  - having problems copying from the board;
  - frequent eye flickers as they read.
- Try making transparent overlays available in classrooms for children to use if they feel the need. Most children will want to try out a variety of colours, but some children will return again and again to the same colour and you may notice that their reading improves when they use the overlay.

Sorting letters

Put a selection of similar magnetic letters on a tray (for example, *b* and *d*; *a* and *u*; *j* and *y*). Check that the same letter is not always the same colour.

- Use a stopwatch to see how long it takes the child to sort the letters correctly.
- Mix them up.
- Can the child beat their own time?

Encourage the child to use both hands while they are sorting the letters. This will increase their speed but also activate more parts of their brain.

Once children are good at this activity:

- Mix three different letters (for example, *d*, *b*, *h*; or *j*, *y*, *g*).
- Mix photocopies of letter patterns (for example, *ir*, *er*; *oi*, *ow*).
- Mix photocopies of words (for example, *can*, *come*; *for*, *from*; *it*, *is*).

Minimal pairs

A minimal pair is a pair of words that sound the same except for one letter: *cat*, *sat*; *cat*, *cap*; *cat*, *cut* are all minimal pairs.

- Download free images from the internet to illustrate minimal pairs. Make all of the pairs minimal in the same way (for example, vary only the first letter, or only the middle letter, or only the final letter).
- Let children work in pairs: one says a word and the other has to identify the appropriate picture.

When children are able to do this well:

- Put out a selection of three pictures. Say one member of a minimal pair; can the children work out which of the pictures shows the other member?

Good listening

- Teach children the signs of active listening:
  - eyes looking at the speaker;
  - mouth closed;
  - body and hands still (or at least not doing anything that interferes with listening);
  - listening ears.

Riddles

Find a book of simple riddles to share, ideally one with picture support.

- Teach children how to listen to the clues.
- Ask children to explain how they arrived at the answer each time.

Aspect 2: Visual and auditory perception and memory

Aspect 2: Visual and auditory perception and memory

Letters	Visual perception	Visual memory	Auditory perception	Auditory memory	P scale/ NC level
I	Counts up to ten objects moving eyes only	Remembers details from a picture and reproduces them on a second picture	Recognises how a sentence is spoken (*happily*, *angrily*, *scarily* and so on)	Listens to a short story/explanation to find the answer to a question	1
I	Identifies several examples of an individual word in a paragraph of text	Has strategies for remembering orientation of *b*, *d*, *p*, *q* as well as numerals		Maintains focus on a teacher-given task for 10 minutes	
J	Follows pathway through a simple maze using eyes only	Remembers the order of letters in most long vowel phonemes	Answers simple questions within 5 seconds of peers	Recites days of the week	2
J	Distinguishes visually similar words (e.g. *grown*, *ground*; *saw*, *was*; *for*, *of*)	Reproduces a sequence of five letters, numbers or symbols	Articulates all common sounds in words appropriately	Returns to an interrupted activity and continues without redirection	
K	Identifies individual objects in a complex picture	Plays Kim's game with up to six objects		Repeats instructions, having listened to a class introduction	2
K	Says the whole word when reading – does not omit beginning or end sounds	Copies a sentence accurately from a card	Correctly pronounces all syllables in common three-syllable words	Follows classroom instructions to complete a three-step task appropriately	
L	Enjoys *Where's X?* pictures where there is some complexity	Spells at least 200 tricky high- and medium-frequency words	Correctly pronounces adjacent consonants (e.g. *st*op, *sa*nd, *street*)	Remembers 2, 5, 10 times tables	
L	Identifies syllable boundaries in long words	Spells longer words by remembering the spelling of each syllable	Reads and pronounces two- or three-syllable nonsense words accurately	Maintains focus for 15 minutes of teacher talk	

Suggested activities

Estimation

- Teach children to count objects using their eyes only. Introduce strategies for telling which items have been counted.
- Gradually increase the difficulty of the task from counting objects in straight lines to counting random patterns of objects.
- Once children are able to count, talk about estimation using eyes only.
- Teach them to count after they have estimated.

Orientation

Many dyslexic children struggle to remember order and orientation of letters, numbers and symbols. Use wooden or plastic letters and numbers initially, but then introduce more abstract symbols which you can draw or generate on a computer using symbolic alphabets and fonts (for example, Wingdings).

- Begin by offering opportunities to match by placing one object directly on top of another. Simple posting boxes and peg jigsaws can help with this level of activity.
- When children can match one object on top, ask them to match directly underneath. Gradually introduce more similar symbols which differ by size and orientation only.
- Build the difficulty by placing two or more symbols together in a sequence for children first to match, then to remember and reproduce.

'Take-up time'

Children with auditory processing difficulties need more 'take-up time' than their peers. Try counting inside your head for up to 10 or 20 seconds before pressing for an answer. If the child does not answer in that time:

- Tell the child that you will expect them to answer the next question so they should listen carefully.
- Ask an easy question which you are confident they will be able to answer.
- Be prepared to wait. Many children with auditory processing difficulties learn to 'opt out' of whole-class teaching time and soon stop listening and learning.
- Warn the rest of the class that they need not put their hands up, because you know that this child knows the answer.
- Once you have established an expectation of the child's participation in the lesson, continue to allow additional 'take-up time'.
- Away from the whole class, talk to the child and explain that they are going to work with you to reduce the additional 'take-up time'.

Following a sequence of instructions

Talk to the child about what helps them to remember. Is it images? Words? Actions? Give them experience of trying to remember a sequence of three instructions using different strategies. Which strategies are most successful?

- Once the child has decided which strategies work best for them, give them practice of using those strategies in a range of different contexts. Is the same strategy successful in all of the contexts?

Barrier tasks

Give two children exactly the same equipment and place a barrier between them. One child should tell the other how to create something using the equipment. The instructor needs to be very explicit; the other child needs to listen carefully, ask questions to clarify, and follow the instructions. Barrier tasks can include activities such as:

- Colour a picture. (Provide two identical line drawings and the same coloured pencils.)
- Create a pattern. (Provide identical sets of coloured beads, pegs, or cubes.)
- Build a structure. (Provide identical sets of building bricks.)
- Place items on a grid. (Initially, make each square on the grid a different colour so that children do not need to worry about 'right' and 'left'.)
- Put features on a pirate map. (Ensure that there are some features to use as the basis for instructions.)

Aspect 2: Visual and auditory perception and memory

Letters	Visual perception	Visual memory	Auditory perception	Auditory memory	P scale/ NC level
M	Looks for similarities in spellings for related words (e.g. *happy, happiness; busy, business*)	Copies short paragraphs accurately from a card	Follows three instructions within 5 seconds of peers	Identifies the 'main idea' of 5 minutes of teacher talk	2
M	Estimates appropriately up to 40 objects	Copies one or two sentences from the board		Uses a mind map to record key ideas while teacher is talking	
N	Estimates appropriately up to 50 objects	Copies two or more paragraphs accurately from a card	Follows instructions in line with peers	Remembers all times tables	3
N				Works out how long it is until a given event using days of the week or months of the year	

54 *The Target Ladders*
© *Target Ladders: Dyslexia* LDA Permission to Photocopy

Suggested activities

Spelling

When first introducing words, it is better not to introduce confusable words at the same time: allow one to become securely learned before introducing the second.

When you do introduce the second word:

- Draw attention to the important differences between the two words (for example, *brought* and *bought*).
- Talk about the different meanings.
- Make links to related words (for example, *bring*, *buy*).
- Discuss ways of remembering which word is which (for example, *bring* and *brought* both begin with *br*).

Copying

There are some occasions when children need to copy from a card or a board, although these occasions should be minimised. Do this only for the most important reasons.

- Make sure that children know what they are copying. If they cannot read it independently, read it to them. (But consider whether or not it is important that they should copy something that they cannot read.)
- Use colour. Either place different coloured dots at the beginning and end of each line or write in a different colour. This allows children to return to the relevant line each time.
- Ensure that the lines of text are appropriately spaced.
- Allow additional time – this will be stressful for dyslexic children.
- Check the accuracy of what has been copied.

Mind mapping

Dyslexic children generally have a better visual memory than auditory memory – and mind mapping combines both visual and auditory to use all of a child's strengths.

When teaching children to mind map:

- Start by modelling the process. Either:
  - create a mind map and then use it to explain what you know about a subject; or
  - create the mind map with the class in the course of a lesson.
- Then let children work in pairs in order that they can embed their understanding through discussion as they record.
- Structure the lesson with regular pauses between each 'topic' to allow for discussion about what to record and where to record it.
- Make it clear what you want the children to achieve, for example, three main topics and two facts about each one.
- Once children have mastered the basics of mind mapping, encourage them to use the technique and to adapt it. For example, they can draw pictures, use colour or use simple mind mapping programmes on the computer.
- If you have an exam or test, help children to construct mind maps as part of their revision.

Alphabetical order

Once children know the alphabet, teach them to write it (or use plastic letters to construct it) in a rainbow shape with *l*, *m*, *n* at the peak of the curve. This will help them to visualise where each letter occurs in the alphabet.

- Name letters out of sequence and ask children to write or place letters in their correct position.
- Name five letters and ask children to put them into alphabetical order, then to tell you which letter comes before or after the ones you initially mentioned.

Teach children about the 'quartiles' of a dictionary: *a–d*, *e–m*, *n–r*, *s–z*.

- Ask children to open the dictionary half way and predict which initial letter they will find.
- Ask them to open the dictionary at *d*. They will have to use the quartiles to see if they can just open the dictionary at *d* without turning over any pages.

Aspect 2: Visual and auditory perception and memory

Aspect 3: Phonics and spelling

Letters	Reading with phonics	Reading tricky words	Spelling with phonics	Tricky words and spelling rules	P scale/ NC level
A	Listens to and repeats initial sound in familiar names and words	Selects own name from a selection of two	Records some letter sounds and symbols associated with own name		P5
A	Identifies dominant sound in a 'tongue-twister' (e.g. *Lucy likes lemon lollipops*)	Matches short words to words under pictures			
B	Recognises ten letters by sound	Says another word beginning with the same sound as their name	Mostly uses letter forms when mark-making	Writes own name	P6
B	Recognises 19 letters by sound	Recognises a few familiar words			
C	Recognises all letters of the alphabet by sound	Recognises familiar captions around the classroom	Begins to use some letter sounds in writing	Writes one or two simple words from memory	P7
C	Hears and identifies initial sounds in words	Recognises first ten high-frequency words	Initial sounds of words often represented in writing		
D	Hears and identifies final and middle sounds in words	Recognises first 30 high-frequency words	More than one sound in a word is generally represented	Writes up to five simple words from memory	P8
D	Blends letters to read VC words (e.g. *it, am*) and CVC words (e.g. *can, pit*)	Begins to recognise known words in different contexts	Orally segments CVC words and writes at least initial and final sounds	Spells CVC words from own writing	

56 *The Target Ladders*

© Target Ladders: Dyslexia   LDA   Permission to Photocopy

Suggested activities

Multi-sensory phonics

Many dyslexic children (particularly those with an auditory processing difficulty) struggle to learn phonics, but the evidence suggests that you need to persevere with teaching phonics because it is an important tool in both spelling and reading.

Dyslexic children will benefit from a systematic, structured, cumulative, multi-sensory approach to learning phonics. Phonics and spelling are ideal subjects to introduce using multi-sensory activities: use plastic, foam or wooden letters; use different coloured card to represent different types of word; create silly sayings together; ask children to make a physical response (jump, stand, stick your tongue out ... and so on) to particular stimuli; be creative.

Alliterative sentences

Children love playing with language and making up silly sentences.

- Model making them up yourself, based on the children's names: *Sarah saw a silly sausage. Reda reads red writing.*
- Once children have got the idea of the silly sentences, try introducing words which are out of place and see if the children can identify the wrong word, for example: *Callum can kiss a giraffe.* Suggest a better word: *Callum can kiss a kangaroo.*
- Provide a bank of pictures of people or creatures, of verbs and of some adjectives such as colours. Write the initial letter of each picture under it to help children to collect the same sound.
- Can children work together to put their pictures in order to make a silly sentence?

Word hunt

Introduce tricky words through a word hunt.

- Write individual words (mostly known with one or two new words) on separate pieces of card. Tell the child what all of the words are.
- Ask the child to read the words back to you.
- Make a wall of the words the child recognises. Play games and talk about the words they do not recognise.
- Stick the words up around the classroom. Can children find, for example, *the*, *here*, *my*?
- Hide the words in a sand tray, or write them on waterproof plastic and put them in water. Challenge the child to find the word, for example, *the*, *here*, *my*.

Dictations

For some children, it is appropriate to separate the writing processes of composition from those of recording. Composition can be done with a scribe, or an audio-recording device. For a short time, the beginner writer may benefit from only writing to dictation. Advantages of this approach are:

- The writer is focused only on spelling and handwriting; they do not have to remember any longer text.
- The dictation can be constructed such that it only requires graphemes that the child has been taught. In this way, there is a clear expectation that the child knows how to record each word.
- It underlines the use of phonics for spelling and provides an opportunity to practise the phonics that has been recently taught.
- New 'tricky words' can be taught and then practised in the context of dictations.

Children who are going through this process should only ever be asked to write to dictation until their knowledge of phonics is secure and advanced. Otherwise, their confidence that they should be able to write each word they want to spell can be shaken.

'Magic lines'

For some children 'magic lines' are a useful aid when they are beginning to use their sounds in writing. Children who are worried about getting their spelling wrong can be shown how to use a short horizontal line to represent the sounds in a word they do not feel able to write.

Aspect 3: Phonics and spelling

Letters	Reading with phonics	Reading tricky words	Spelling with phonics	Tricky words and spelling rules	NC level
E	Recognises some vowel digraphs in isolation	Uses phonics cues beyond the first sound to predict words, including tricky words	Segments a CVC word then writes all letters recognisably	Knows that *ll, ss, ck* occur at the end of words	1
E	Blends CVC words containing known vowel and consonant digraphs (e.g. *sheep*, *rain*)	Recognises 50 high-frequency words	Uses known graphemes to attempt to write words using phonic strategies	Writes up to 30 high-frequency words including 6 tricky words	
F	Hears and identifies adjacent consonants in words (e.g. *flag*, *sand*)	Reads a range of simple words and sentences independently	Uses phonic knowledge to write simple, regular words	Writes up to 50 high-frequency words including 18 tricky words	1
F	Looks at a picture of a CVCC word (e.g. *sand*) or CCVC word (e.g. *frog*) and says the sounds	Recognises 75 high-frequency words		Adds 's' to make a plural	
F	Looks beyond single letters to find known graphemes in words	Identifies the 'tricky bit' when reading a word	Knows at least one way of representing all phonemes in English	Identifies the 'tricky bit' when spelling a word	
F	Uses phonic knowledge to attempt to read unfamiliar words	Uses known letter patterns as a strategy to work out a tricky word	Uses knowledge of vowel digraphs when writing simple words	Uses phonic knowledge to attempt to spell topic words in writing	
H	Knows some alternative pronunciations for common letter patterns	Reliably blends known pronunciations of graphemes to read unknown words	Writes some CVC words with long vowel phonemes (e.g. *rain*, *sheep*) accurately	Spells up to 30 tricky words	1
H	Uses elements from known words to work out unknown words	Recognises 100 high-frequency words	Records both sounds in adjacent consonants	Spells words for numbers up to 20	

Suggested activities

Reading to the end of a word

For many children, there is a reading barrier when they begin to read words with vowel digraphs: they are used to 'sounding out' by saying each letter sound and do not recognise digraphs.

- Talk about the need to read through to the end of a word. This is particularly important for words with split digraphs (for example, *made*), those with a suffix or inflection at the end (for example, *laughing*) and multi-syllabic words (for example, *crocodile*).
- When you teach vowel digraphs, always teach them in the context of words rather than in isolation. Initially, colour them in the word so that their shape stands out, but as soon as possible present the digraph as part of the word.

Recognising and writing

Don't let writing the graphemes drag behind reading them: teach both processes together. As soon as children learn a grapheme, they should be expected to spell it in individual words and encouraged to try it out in independent writing.

- Let the child keep a record of graphemes they know, those they are practising and those they have met for the first time. Encourage self-assessment as the child maintains their own record.
- Once sounds are known, they can be transferred onto a chart as a reminder for writing.

Saying the sounds

Whether segmenting to spell or blending to read, the child needs to understand the relationship between the aural/vocal sounds and their graphic representations.

- When children are spelling, teach them to 'stretch' the word in order to hear each of the sounds eg *ss-t-rr-eee-tch*. Often, this is easier as a whisper. Once the child has said the sounds, and counted them, they can then focus on representing them.

- 'Phoneme frames' or 'sound strings' are often used to help children to ensure that all of the sounds are represented. If the child has counted five sounds, they know they will need to represent five sounds. Many of the sounds in a word are uncontentious, but in most words there is at least one choice to be made (for example, is the final sound in stretch represented with *ch* or *tch*?) At this point, children either need to think about spelling rules they know, or they should write the word with both spellings and see which one 'looks right'.

Table top writing mat

Since dyslexic children have to pay close attention to spelling, they often struggle to write high-quality texts because they cannot remember everything and spelling often takes precedence over the choice of vocabulary and sentence structure. Reduce the spelling memory load by providing a bank of words.

- Use the outside edges of a piece of laminated A3 paper. Leave the space in the middle blank for the child's exercise book.
- On the right hand side, create a list of common words that the child is currently learning.
- Along the top, include a chart showing all of the different ways the child is learning to represent each sound.
- Down the left, write words which the child will need for this activity: topic words, connectives, sentence starters and so on.

Aspect 3: Phonics and spelling

Letters	Reading with phonics	Reading tricky words	Spelling with phonics	Tricky words and spelling rules	NC level
I	Knows some alternative representations for common letter patterns	Recognises 150 high- and medium-frequency words	Knows alternative ways of representing some common graphemes	Uses phonic knowledge to spell more adventurous words	2
I	Blends known graphemes to read two- and three-syllable words	Recognises that phonics is part of a 'toolkit' of strategies to read unfamiliar words	Errors show some recall of letter patterns and known graphemes	Many common words spelt correctly	
J	Knows different common representations of many graphemes	Tries out all known pronunciations of letter patterns as a strategy for making meaning	Knows alternative ways of representing many graphemes	Spells irregular plural forms with some accuracy	2
J	Knows different common pronunciations of many graphemes	Recognises 200 high- and medium-frequency words	Spells longer words by remembering the spelling of each syllable	Knows rules for adding *ing* to verbs and sometimes uses them in writing	
K	Scans to the end of a word in order to check for digraphs or trigraphs	Notices spelling patterns in unfamiliar words and applies them to new words	Spells common grammatical function words correctly	Looks for similarities in spellings for related words	2
K	Reads without sounding out aloud	'Solves' most words in a 'levelled' text with little difficulty		Incorrect spellings show some awareness of word structure (e.g. includes *ing* and *ed*)	
L	Tackles multi-syllabic words with confidence	Recognises many common suffixes and prefixes	Makes plausible attempts to spell longer and less common words	Spells common grammatical function words	3
L	Effectively uses a range of strategies to read with fluency, understanding and meaning			Makes phonetically plausible attempts to spell multi-syllabic words	

60 *The Target Ladders*

Suggested activities

Reading syllables

By the time they are reading at this level, children should be able to tackle multi-syllabic words.

- Confirm that in English, a syllable must contain a vowel sound (which may be represented by *y* in some contexts) and may also contain consonants.
- Ask children to identify the syllable boundaries. There is a lot of dispute about precisely where the boundary falls, so accept a reasonable approximation (for example, *com-put-er*; *comp-u-ter* but not *co-mpu-ter* since *mp* does not appear at the beginning of a word or syllable in English).
- Ask them to work out the syllables, then combine the syllables and say the word.

Using rimes

Make use of children's tendency to make links in order to establish groups of analogous words (for example, *drain, rain, pain, grain* but *bake, cake, drake, fake*).

- Use word lists and ask children to sort the words according to spelling patterns.
- Ask them to act as detectives and write spelling 'rules', using what they observe.
- Remind children that English is a tricky language so most rules have exceptions and can be broken, but at least the 'rules' will create a starting point.

Long and short vowels

In order for children to learn many spelling rules, they must first learn to distinguish between long and short vowels.

- There are six short vowel sounds in standard southern English (but check for the accents your children use). They are the vowel sounds in *pat, pet, pit, pot, putt, put*.
- All other vowel sounds in monosyllabic words are long vowels. In standard southern English they are the vowel sounds in: *bait, beat, bite, boat, boot, bought, bird, bard, beard, bow, boy, bear*.
- Schwa is always an unstressed vowel. It is the sound at the end of *butter* and *colour*, at the beginning of *alone* and in the middle of *crocodile*.
- It is important to remember that the letter patterns are not important: it is the vowel sound that matters (for example, *ea* represents a long vowel in *bead* but a short vowel in *head*).

Digraph bingo

Play card games such as bingo, memory games, Happy Families and Lotto in order to reinforce graphemes which represent the same phoneme. For many children this learning is hard to master and the aim for a dyslexic child is that this knowledge should be automatic and easily accessible.

- Teach families of digraphs (for example, *wait, plate, eight, straight, may, they, apron*). Discuss which spelling pattern is most likely in different contexts.
- Write the words on individual cards and use the digraph in context as you play the games.
- Individual children may benefit from having their own version of the game to play at odd moments of the day.

Aspect 3: Phonics and spelling

Letters	Reading with phonics	Reading tricky words	Spelling with phonics	Tricky words and spelling rules	NC level
M	Uses phonic, contextual, graphic and syntactical cues with greater ease	Uses knowledge of suffixes and prefixes to swiftly decode and understand unfamiliar words	Knows when to double a letter before adding a suffix or inflection	Is learning and applying more advanced spelling rules	3
M			Spells most words, including 'topic' words, correctly	Knows rules for adding *ed* and *ing* to verbs	
N		Begins to make some use of related words when working out the meaning of unfamiliar words		Knows rules for adding suffixes to words ending in *y*	3

The Target Ladders

Suggested activities

Spelling rules

Spelling rules are useful, although exceptions can invariably be found to most rules. Spelling rules are most useful if children find them out through activities and understanding, rather than if they are simply learned and parroted.

- Start with reading: challenge children to look for (for example) words ending in '*ed*' in a passage of text.
- Once they have found and listed the words, ask children to sort them. The sorting could take different forms depending on your focus: according to how the *ed* is pronounced or according to whether or not there is a double letter in the word. Or ask children to sort the words according to their own criteria and see what they come up with.
- Once the children have sorted the words, ask them to explain what they have found. You may need to help them to create a short and memorable explanation.

Look, say, cover, write, check

Although many schools claim to use this approach to teaching spelling, it is rarely used effectively.

- 'Look' is the most important part of the process. It is not a brief glance but an active, engaged process, which may include:
  - discussion about patterns observed, similarities to other words and so on;
  - identification of the tricky bit of the word;
  - finger tracing of the tricky bit;
  - discussion of any visual aspects of the word that make it memorable;
  - finding words within words.
- 'Say' is another important part of the process. It helps to anchor the child's attention; it provides an auditory memory to combine with the visual one.
- 'Cover' means to cover the word up. While it is covered, ask the child to visualise the word. Looking up and to the left is often helpful while the child tries to visualise what the word looks like.
- 'Write' provides the kinaesthetic 'muscle memory' of the word. If the child knows cursive handwriting, or any joined up handwriting, it is useful to use it at this point to help to reinforce the kinaesthetic memories.
- 'Check' shows that it is the learner's responsibility to ensure that the spelling matches the target.

To make the process more powerful, ask children to return to the word list after an hour and repeat it with a much briefer look at the words. How many did they manage to get right this time?

Sound it out

For dyslexic children, it continues to be important to 'say the sounds' when they are writing tricky or unfamiliar words. This helps to promote a multi-sensory memory of the words, but it also reduces the likelihood of swapping the order of letters or missing them out entirely.

Aspect 3: Phonics and spelling

Aspect 4: Reading comprehension and fluency

Letters	Engaging with print; reading with fluency	Reading with meaning	Using inference	Understanding structure; responding to the book	P scale/ NC level
A	Draws finger from left to right under text, unrelated to adult reading	Enjoys listening to stories; remembers the name of a character	Makes predictions in simple, familiar texts	Turns pages from beginning to end	P4
A	Looks at left hand page before right hand page	Talks about events and characters in a story or pictures in a non-fiction book	Participates in role-play related to a story	Joins in with sequencing objects, pictures or actions related to a story or recount	
B	Matches objects to pictures and symbols	'Reads' single words labelling pictures or photographs in non-fiction books	Can say if a character is 'kind' or 'bad' in a familiar story	Joins in with actions as a familiar story is read or told	P5
B	Matches objects to pictures and symbols	Points to picture to answer simple questions	Through role-play, demonstrates understanding of the link between a character and an action	Joins in with repeated phrases as a familiar book is re-read	
C	Knows that a familiar word such as *cat* always says the same, in a book, on a display and so on	'Reads' back own mark-making, saying words in response to marks on page	Uses a familiar story, poem or non-fiction book as the basis for role-play	Tells a story from memory, using pictures for sequence	P6
C	Matches short words	Pretends to read environmental print	Points to a picture of the main character	Uses some book language when retelling part of a story	
D	Reads familiar captions with 1-1 correspondence	Predicts missing words in a sentence or familiar refrain	Takes on known characters in role-play	Understands simple story language such as *title*, *characters*, *beginning* and *end*	P7
D	Points to individual words as they are read aloud from left to right	'Reads back' own writing with 1-1 correspondence	Links events in books to own experience	Knows the sequence of events in a book and can 'Find the place where ...'	

Suggested activities

Matching and sequencing

At the very beginning, reading involves matching, sequencing and memory. Matching and sequencing tasks are therefore important for children who are at the earliest stages of beginning to read.

- Provide activities such as:
  - matching images, shapes, symbols;
  - matching a photograph to an object;
  - matching symbols to photographs or objects;
  - continuing a simple pattern (for example, red, green, red, green, red ...) or a more complex pattern (for example, red, green, yellow, red ... or blue, blue, green, blue, blue ...);
  - completing jigsaws;
  - matching and sorting tactile letter shapes;
  - finding all the iterations of a letter in a page of print;
  - finding as many different sizes, colours and variations of one letter in a newspaper or magazine as they can;
  - matching short words.

Inferring meaning

Although inference is always deemed to be a 'higher order reading skill' it is in fact something which children do from the time they begin to make sense of their world. You can encourage the development of the skill in pre-literate children using pictures, either from picture books for younger children or from Grand Masters in online art galleries. You need to be prepared to divide your questions about the pictures into two sorts: 'it's there' (direct evidence), and 'what do you think?' (which are questions which encourage inference and check on understanding of language).

'It's there' questions include questions which begin:

- How many ...?
- What can you see ....?
- What is he wearing/holding/looking at ...?

'What do you think' question starters include:

- How is he going to ...?
- Where is she going ...?
- What happened just before this scene?
- What do you think will happen next?
- Why do you think they're ...?
- What time of day is it?
- How do you think she feels about ...?

After each question, follow up with a 'How do you know?', 'What makes you say that?' type of question to teach children the importance of producing evidence to back up their opinions.

Enjoying books

Reading can be a very social activity, as the number of book clubs for adults demonstrates. No matter what age the child, encourage them to enjoy the experience of shared reading.

- Activities could involve:
  - hearing a story read aloud;
  - participating in the reading;
  - talking about what happened in the story;
  - making links between the child's own life and something in the book;
  - looking at pictures in non-fiction books to ask and answer questions;
  - comparing pictures in different books to combine the information found;
  - sharing a comic or Manga with a friend;
  - sharing a puzzle book in which the answers are visual.

There are increasing numbers of high-quality information books being produced, which rely more on the pictures than on text. These can be particularly popular with older children who find reading hard.

Aspect 4: Reading comprehension and fluency

Letters	Engaging with print; reading with fluency	Reading with meaning	Using inference	Understanding structure; responding to the book	P scale/ NC level
E	Identifies full stop and question mark in text	Expects written text to make sense; uses pictures for 'sense checks'	Identifies what a book is about	Identifies likely subject matter of a book by looking at the cover illustrations	P8
E	Matches writing and known words to read environmental print	Reads simple, decodable texts and falters if they do not make sense	Identifies the main character(s) and events in a book	Sequences pictures to retell a story	
F	Points to punctuation marks in text	Uses pictures to answer simple questions about a text that they have read, not heard	With support and modelling, makes some predictions about how a story they are reading might end	Uses small world sets or puppets to re-enact a story they have read	1
F	Uses pictures and context to help with decoding	Answers simple questions about a non-fiction text	Finds a selection of books which are about the same subject	Draws pictures while retelling a story	
G	Talks about significant features of the layout (e.g. when the text has been enlarged, stretched and so on for emphasis)	Can answer *who, what, when, where* questions about a story they have read	With some support, can make predictions about how a character may act or is feeling	Locates and reads a significant point in the book	1
G	May substitute plausible attempts at words based on context and picture cues	Can answer *who, what, when, where* questions about a non-fiction book they have enjoyed	Uses pictures to discuss or elaborate on the setting	Identifies the main points in the correct sequence	
H	Begins to use some expression when re-reading familiar books	Answers simple questions using specific details in the book	Uses pictures to identify who said what in a story they have read	Knows that some books have stories and others have information and instructions	1
H	Understands how emphasis is created through simple text features (e.g. font size)	Identifies a favourite character or event and locates the image in a book they are reading	Answers questions about the impact of different aspects of the book (e.g. title, cover, illustrations)	With support, identifies a favourite book or a favourite part of a book and explains the choice	

The Target Ladders

© *Target Ladders: Dyslexia*   LDA   Permission to Photocopy

Suggested activities

Fluency and punctuation

Teach children how punctuation helps the reader to make sense of the text. Try not to encourage them to make a link between punctuation and breathing. (The way they treat punctuation in reading will influence what they do in writing.)

- Read a page of their book to them using normal intonation.
- Ask them to indicate when they 'hear' any punctuation marks.
- Help them to think about what they heard in your voice. Normally, your intonation goes slightly down at the end of a sentence, and you do pause although you don't necessarily breathe. If the sentence ends with a question mark, the intonation tends to rise.
- Ask the child to re-read the page to you, demonstrating their awareness of punctuation marks.
- As they read a bit more text, encourage fluency. Once the child has read a sentence, working out the words, ask them to re-read it fluently so the child gets used to hearing their own voice reading fluently.
- Always aim for fluency, even when the child is reading very simple books.

Making meaning

In the very best picture books, including many books in reading schemes, the pictures give additional information to the text, often telling a slightly different story. Children reading at this level tend to make meaning by combining information from text and image, although up to about 10 per cent of readers find this challenging and can focus on only one medium at a time.

- Encourage awareness of both text and picture, but if a child cannot combine the two, read the book from the text first, then you re-read it while the child looks at the pictures for the additional information.
- From the beginning, encourage children to use their ears when they read so that they can tell if they are not making sense. Self-monitoring is an important skill, which should be taught as early as possible.
- Help children to develop individual strategies which indicate that something has gone wrong: re-reading the sentence, pausing, looking at you to ask for help ... any of these is acceptable as long as they are initiated by the child.

Using inference

Once children are used to inferring ideas from 'What do you think ...' questions based on pictures, encourage them to transfer the skill to listening to books read aloud.

- Role-play in response to a story they have heard is a powerful medium for inferential questions.
- Read simple play scripts together. These are wonderful for inference since there is no narrative to tell how people are feeling or what they might do next.
- Develop children's understand of vocabulary used to talk about a book: *characters*, *setting*, *plot*, *title*, *chapter*, *paragraph*, *heading*, *subheading*, *caption*, *index*, *contents*.
- Use non-fiction books as part of your work together. Ask children to make choices about which books they use to find out about particular topics.

Sequencing ideas

Digital cameras are very useful for creating simple sequences which can then be the basis of retelling a story or ordering ideas.

- Take photographs of role-play or puppets or small world people. Ask children to identify the important photographs, sequence them and retell the story.
- Take photographs of activities such as cooking, constructions or DT projects. Ask children to identify the important photographs, sequence them and explain what they show.

Aspect 4: Reading comprehension and fluency

Letters	Engaging with print; reading with fluency	Reading with meaning	Using inference	Understanding structure; responding to the book	NC level
I	Uses appropriate intonation and pauses briefly at full stops in familiar texts	Recalls the main idea and locates it in a familiar book with some independence	Makes simple predictions with some independence	Explains the difference between fiction and non-fiction texts	2
I	With some support, reads fluently rather than from word to word	Finds information in the text in response to a question	Makes links from a book they have read independently to their own experience	Talks about similarities and differences with other books they have read	
J	Generally takes account of end of sentence punctuation (full stop, question mark, exclamation mark) when reading	Recalls main story ideas, explaining how events link together	Uses experience of other texts as the basis for making predictions	With some support, explains the main features of non-fiction books	2
J	Often self-corrects if the reading does not make sense	Says what they have found out when reading a non-fiction book	Begins to find words or details in pictures which show how a character is feeling	Identifies particular words or phrases which add to the impact on the reader	
K	Reads with some expression, taking account of common punctuation	Can generate own questions about a text, based on adult models	With some help, can draw, act or describe a character's feelings	Compares structure, organisation and layout with other texts	2
K	Gains overall impression of a text by scanning cover, title, blurb and so on	Is efficient when finding the place in a book which gives evidence about an idea, character, event or topic	Understands that some stories have a message or a moral	Responds to a text by discussing other texts they have read with similar themes, subjects, characters and so on	
L	Always self-corrects if the reading does not make sense	Begins to identify the main points or information gleaned from a paragraph	Responds to and discusses a character's feelings, finding words and phrases from the text	Identifies powerful words and phrases and discusses their impact	3
L	Begins to 'read ahead' to support reading with expression	Evaluates usefulness of information read in a variety of non-fiction texts	Uses relevant information from a text in research activities	Understands and explains features of layout in non-fiction texts	

Suggested activities

Summarising

Many dyslexic children find it hard to summarise a passage, reporting only on the key points. They do not always identify the same main points as you might.

- Begin by modelling the process, presenting your summary in a chart. The use of this visual is important, as is the small size of the cells: information will need to be prioritised to fit. The chart could be as simple as this:

Title	Event	Key points
The Wolf	Eats grandmother	○ Knocks on door ○ Eats grandmother ○ Dresses in her nightie and gets into bed

Title	Information	Key points
Volcanoes	Why they are where they are	○ At the edges of tectonic plates ○ Under sea and on land ○ Undersea volcanoes can cause tsunamis ○ Volcanoes are often in earthquake zones

- Initially, fill in the first two columns together while the child tries to find no more than three or four points to complete the final column.

Scanning

Explain that scanning is about finding individual words or phrases in a text.

- Write the alphabet at the top of a page of print. Ask the child to scan the words on the page, looking for each letter in turn. They should circle the first *a*, then the next *b* then the next *c* and so on. The letters the child circles should replicate the order of the alphabet at the top of the page. (It is easiest to create your own text of nonsense words and ensure that all of the letters of the alphabet are on the page.)
- Write a list of high-frequency words that you know are on the page. Ask the child to circle all of the words.
- Identify a word which appears several times on a page (often with different endings) and ask the child to circle all of the words.

Skimming

Explain that skimming is about trying to get the main idea of a passage or pages without reading every word carefully.

- Ask the child to look at your eyes while you model the process. They should see how quickly your eyes move as they skim over the text.
- Identify a precise research question to which you want to find an answer.
- Ask the child to read a paragraph to see if it contains the answer. Time their reading and watch their eyes.
- Did the paragraph contain the answer? If so, ask the child to re-read the paragraph properly to find the answer. If not, identify another paragraph to skim read.

Using the internet

Much of a young person's 'research' these days will be done via the internet. Dyslexic children, in particular, will benefit from being explicitly taught e-literacy.

- Ensure that they understand the school's safe internet usage policy, why it is in place and how vulnerable children can be online. Take them to http://www.thinkuknow.co.uk to explore different aspects of e-safety.
- Show children how to read a web page.
  - Can they distinguish text from adverts?
  - Show them where to start reading on a busy page.
  - Can they identify how the page creates headings, subheadings and so on?
  - Do they know how to identify and to follow hyperlinks?
  - Can they follow their 'breadcrumb trail' to get back to where they started their search?
- Clarify the procedure for reporting anything that makes them feel insecure at http://ceop.police.uk/.

Aspect 4: Reading comprehension and fluency

Letters	Engaging with print; reading with fluency	Reading with meaning	Using inference	Understanding structure; responding to the book	NC level
M	Reads aloud expressively, responding to a wider range of punctuation marks	With support, comments include direct reference to, and quotations from, the text	Suggests a character's motivations for their actions	Uses knowledge of text type and layout to retrieve information efficiently	3
M	Reads with sustained concentration	Explanations of events can be linked to personal experience	With support, is able to identify the point of view from which a story or non-fiction text has been written	Gives an overview of a text and offers a personal response	
N	Consistently reads with expression, using a voice which is appropriate to the text	Begins to support a comment using ideas or information from more than one place in a text	Discusses characters' feelings and motivations using evidence from the text	Uses technical vocabulary (*adjective*, *adverb*, *simile*) to explain the impact and efficacy of descriptive writing	3
N	Reads longer and more challenging texts with sustained concentration	Can skim, scan and make notes to support oral summary of the content of a passage	Finds words and phrases in the text to support interpretation of events or ideas in a text	Scans contents pages and indexes to evaluate usefulness of a book to current research interest	

The Target Ladders

© *Target Ladders: Dyslexia*   LDA   Permission to Photocopy

Suggested activities

Comprehension monitoring

This skill is critical as children become more fluent, but does not develop naturally or easily in many children. We can all lose track and suddenly realise that we have read a page without taking in anything from it. Children need to develop a 'toolkit' so that they recognise when they have lost focus and they can begin to repair the meaning. They need to learn to:

- be aware of what they are reading;
- know when what they are reading doesn't make sense, or they have lost focus;
- know where in the text this happened so that they can go back and re-read;
- identify the reason for this loss of meaning.
  - Was it because they lost concentration for some reason? In which case, what are they planning to do?
  - Was something in the text confusing? In which case, they need to develop strategies for solving the problem, for example, asking questions, finding out something on the internet or in a dictionary, referring to notes.

Mind mapping

Many dyslexic children have holistic methods of learning, which are not well represented, recorded or remembered from sequential texts or notes. Mind mapping can be used:

- *To make notes in class.* Encourage this by ensuring that you plan your lesson in 'chunks' followed by pauses in order to give the children the opportunity to make a brief record of what you have said using visual and verbal representations.
- *For revision.* Model using a mind map to record key ideas from learning and to show how these ideas link together.
- *For planning.* Teach children how to mind map plans for their writing. Mind maps can show:
  - how ideas can link together in paragraphs for non-fiction writing;
  - different aspects of a character or setting;
  - the stages in a story for narrative writing;
  - ideas and vocabulary for preparing a poem.

Highlighting

Highlighting is a particularly useful tool for dyslexic children because it reduces copying and supports the identification of the main ideas.

- Where it is possible and appropriate, teach children how to highlight to record the main words and phrases so that they can:
  - demonstrate how they achieved a learning objective or success criterion by highlighting their own writing;
  - identify the main points in their notes for revision or planning;
  - highlight key facts in a photocopied document;
  - highlight electronically on pdfs and word processed documents.

Answering comprehension questions

Don't just give children practice in completing comprehension tasks; teach them how to get better so that they are proficient in all stages in the process.

- *Read the question.* Teach children to highlight or underline key words in a question. These will be different for different subject areas. Ensure they know the difference between words like *explain, clarify, describe*.
- *Decide where in the text to look.* Teach children to create a 'mental map' of the text so that they remember where on a page they should look for the answer.
- *Identify the technique to use.* Is this skimming or scanning? How much of the text should be read carefully? Where should you start and finish the careful reading?
- *Re-read the question* to ensure that you have found the answer.
- *Frame the response.* Children need to be taught how to summarise what they have found out concisely and accurately. Use your own 'model answers' and compare them to the children's response.
- *Look at the marks.* Talk about the expectations in terms of length of answer for questions with different marks.

Aspect 5: Writing – handwriting, punctuation, sentences and text

Letters	Handwriting and punctuation	Sentence structure	Text structure	Content and style	P scale/ NC level
A	Uses tripod grip	Indicates direction of text with finger	Participates in shared writing sessions	Makes marks to indicate own name	P4
A	Colours mostly within simple, bold outlines	Dictates two-word captions	Makes marks to indicate writing about a picture	Uses mark-making in role-play activities	
B	Writes some letter-like shapes	Tracks left to right when mark-making	With support, engages in composing a range of writing for different audiences and purposes	Identifies own marks as representing their name	P5
B	Traces over name	With support, combines words or symbols to create a caption	Dictates information to record experiences	Uses word and picture banks to record experiences	
C	Holds writing implement with some control	Dictates caption and may copy under adult's writing	Copy-writes captions, invitations and so on	Copy-writes own name, independently producing a recognisable capital letter	P6
C	Writes random strings of symbols, including letter-like shapes	Combines simple words and symbols from a word bank	With support, can retell event or story using role-play	'Re-reads' own role-play writing	
D	Represents letters appropriately when sounding out words to write	Orders words from left to write	Begins to use some 'story language' when dictating or in role-play	States purpose for own writing	P7
D	Begins to leave spaces between groups of letters	Uses 1-1 correspondence between spoken words and written groups of letters	Retells simple familiar stories in sequence	Contributes ideas to shared writing activities	

72   *The Target Ladders*

© *Target Ladders: Dyslexia*   LDA   Permission to Photocopy

Suggested activities

Pencil grip and seating

Pencil grip is an important part of learning to write. If a pencil grip is uncomfortable, too tight, or too loose, children cannot write comfortably and soon learn to dislike writing. As soon as possible in school, teach children how to sit properly at tables and how to hold a pencil. Bad habits formed early are hard to banish in later years.

- A wide variety of pencil grips is now available to help children of all ages to hold writing implements appropriately. Make use of them for your children. This is a very personal thing, and the same tools will not necessarily be appropriate for all children (or for all adults).
- Teach left-handed children to put their book so that it slants at almost 45 degrees to their bodies. This allows plenty of room for them to write across a page without cramping their handwriting.
- Ensure that left-handed children have plenty of elbow room.

Letter formation

As soon as children are able to use pencils and are ready to start letter formation activities, spend one-to-one time with them ensuring a good pencil grip and proper letter formation.

- Use a wide variety of media for establishing 'muscle memory' for the basic shapes in letter formation: as well as sand, try writing letter shapes in shaving foam, cornflour and water, soap flakes.
- Use letters made out of sandpaper and alphabet roll letters to track the letter shape.
- Teach children to write their name by tracing. Insist on the correct letter formation as they do it. Thereafter, whenever the child attempts to write their name – even on the back of a picture – insist on good letter formation.

Lines or blank paper?

The current recommendation is that children who can write on lined paper should be encouraged to do so. The width between the lines is again something that is personal to each child and should not be regarded as a progression according to age. Throughout the school, encourage children to experiment with the paper they write on and with writing implements: creating a hierarchy of expectation of writing tool and writing paper disadvantages many children. Each adult makes their own decisions – why shouldn't children?

Handwriting books with blue and pink lines are an excellent support for a very brief stage in the development of a child's handwriting. At the time when consistency of letter height and the height of ascenders and descenders is a developmental target, then these books are very useful. Before and after that time there is no purpose in using them.

Making writing fun

From the beginning, make writing fun and show that it is communicative.

- Provide 'themed' writing areas, which give children reasons to write.
- Offer the opportunity for children to write short notes to you – and say you will respond to them. This can support both PHSE and writing (as well as hearing the 'pupil voice'). Use a suggestion box, a pigeonhole, a notice board …

As far as possible, give 'responsibility' and 'ownership' of writing to the child: they need to know what they have written. Simply copying your writing does not give them any ownership of the content or the process.

Aspect 5: Writing – handwriting, punctuation, sentences and text

Letters	Handwriting and punctuation	Sentence structure	Text structure	Content and style	P scale/ NC level
E	Forms some commonly used letters using the correct sequence of movements	Dictates a simple sentence, word by word	Uses appropriate layout for common text types (e.g. lists, instructions)	Confidently uses a range of 'writing' for specific purposes	P8
E	Independently positions paper comfortably	Reorders simple words to form a correct sentence	Discusses what to write ahead of writing it	Writes own name with appropriate use of capital and lower case letters	
F	Forms many letters with accurate sequence of movement	Writing generally tracks from left to write and top to bottom of page	Independently thinks of own text for writing	Writes simple statements which reflect intended meaning	1
F	Often leaves 'finger spaces' between words	Expresses ideas in sentence-like structures	Repeats refrains from stories when retelling events	States purpose for writing	
G	Forms most letters with accurate sequence of movement	Most simple sentences are grammatically accurate	Repeated use of noun or pronoun clarifies connections between ideas	Selects words and phrases which show clear awareness of topic	1
G	Starts a piece of writing with a capital letter	Uses repetitive sentence structures	Writing is two or more sentences long	Uses some descriptive language	
H	Most letters correctly orientated	Sentence structures used match a model text	Uses formulaic phrases from model texts	Text layout and language indicates purpose	1
H	Shows some awareness of full stops and capital letters	Sentences are joined by *and*	Events and ideas are generally in an appropriate order	Writing can be mostly read without need for mediation	

The Target Ladders

© *Target Ladders: Dyslexia*   LDA   Permission to Photocopy

Suggested activities

Reorganising sentences

Re-creating cut-up sentences is a useful activity for children who are at an early stage in the development of writing.

- The child dictates a sentence.
- You scribe the sentence, leaving large spaces between the words.
- You read the sentence aloud.
- The child reads the sentence, word by word. As they read each word, you cut it off the beginning of the sentence. Muddle up all of the words.
- The child then works independently to reorganise the words into the original sentence.
- They then read the sentence back to you.
- The child can either copy the sentence into their writing books, or stick in the words they have sequenced.

Using model non-fiction texts

The use of model texts is important for all children as they begin to develop as writers. Non-fiction texts aimed at early readers tend to be based on captions and short sentences. These are ideal models for children at this stage of writing.

- Agree the topic of a non-fiction text.
- Create a mind map showing the desired content for the child's text.
- Show children how to search for, and download, images online.
- Once the child has found and ordered their images, these can either be printed out as the basis for a handwritten text, or the text can be created on the computer too.
- Revisit the model text and talk about how it can be changed to match the new content the child has found.
- Give the child as much independence as possible as they write.

Remembering all the layers of text

For many dyslexic children, writing is too big and frightening a task and it needs to be broken down into smaller sections in order to be achievable.

- Visual planning sheets, story boards, mind maps and so on can be used to record ideas for the shape of the story and inventive vocabulary to use at the appropriate times.
- 'Talk for writing' (see below) will give children an auditory memory of the rhythm of language and vocabulary that they used when retelling their ideas.
- Recording buttons, or other devices, can be used to record the next part of the text.
- Table top mats showing useful graphemes, high-frequency words and topic words are helpful resources to take the pressure away from correct spelling.

Once the memory load of each of these aspects of writing has been reduced, the child has a better chance of creating a high-quality text.

Talk for writing

All children benefit from talk for writing, but dyslexics benefit more than most. Talk for writing can take many forms:

- Drama, music, art, role-play can be used as part of the generation-of-ideas stage of writing. All of these should be accompanied by discussion to give children the opportunity to develop and shape ideas.
- Guided or paired planning gives children the time to work out the sequence of events and to think about language they might need to use at different points in the story.
- Response partners can be used to give children opportunities to tell their story to another child. This should not be a rambling talk around the idea, but a sharply focused opportunity to talk the writing.

Once children have explored their idea orally, they are in a better position to write – although some will still benefit from making an audio-recording of their entire story, and writing only part of it, or word processing the story on a computer and making corrections and improvements by hand.

Aspect 5: Writing – handwriting, punctuation, sentences and text

Letters	Handwriting and punctuation	Sentence structure	Text structure	Content and style	NC level
I	Lower case letters are correctly formed in a script that will be easy to join	Sentences may be joined by *and* and *then*	Ideas are developed in short sections	Gives some detail to expand upon simple ideas	2
I	Uses full stops and capital letters appropriately in more than one sentence	Uses a mixture of simple and compound sentences	Stories have beginnings, middles and ends	Some evidence of effective word choices	
J	Ascenders and descenders are generally distinguished	Sentences are joined by *but* and *so*	Stories have more than one character and event	Generally communicates information effectively to the reader	2
J	Upper case letters are not found in the middle of words	Tense is generally used appropriately	The style and intention of a text are generally linked	Uses some features of text types appropriately	
K	Use of upper and lower case letters is generally appropriate	Sentences are linked by a wider variety of connectives including time-related words	The order of events in a story or non-fiction text is generally appropriate	Viewpoints may be indicated by comments or questions to the reader	2
K	Makes some use of question marks, exclamation marks and commas in lists	Some variation in sentence openings	Uses pronouns to link characters and events within a section of the text	Some adventurous word choices add to impact	
L	Handwriting is consistently legible and generally neat	Sentences are linked by a wider variety of connectives (e.g. *because*, *although*, *when*)	Clearly distinguishes events or stages	Vocabulary choices are appropriate for the setting	3
L	Handwriting is consistently sized with clear ascenders and descenders	Tense is generally consistent within a text	The ending of a story is clearly related to the events	Uses adjectives and adverbs to add more details	

Suggested activities

Joined writing

By this point, children should be beginning to join their handwriting. Although many children resent the time spent practising handwriting, it does make a difference, particularly if you then insist that something they have been taught is demonstrated during the week in the rest of their writing. If you do not insist, then many children will have print script in their writing books and beautifully joined writing in their handwriting books.

Joining is important:

- It adds movement memory to sight and auditory memories and thus supports spelling.
- It eliminates the use of capital letters in the middle of words.
- It helps children to keep spacing within and between words to a consistent length.
- It enables children to write quickly, fluently and legibly.
- It looks good so children can take a pride in their work.
- It allows them to produce a reasonable amount of work in the time given, without undue strain on the writing hand.

Planning

- Teach children different ways of planning their writing:
  - mind mapping;
  - story boards;
  - flow charts;
  - story mountains; the introduction and setting are fairly flat, but at the beginning of the action the tension begins to mount and the line of the story begins to rise, culminating with the exciting part – the peak of the mountain. The resolution is the downwards slope and the conclusion continues into a horizontal line.
  - planning sheets and planning grids.
- Teach children to use all of the different methods of planning in order that they can learn which ones work best for them.

- Insist that children spend time planning. Dyslexic children in particular benefit from doing the thinking and shaping before the writing, so that they can concentrate on the presentational skills while they write.

Using a laptop

For some children, the use of a laptop (or other word processing device such as an Alphasmart) becomes necessary at around this stage, particularly for children who are also dyspraxic. The laptop helps the children to produce work that reflects their knowledge, content and effort. Advantages of laptops for dyslexic children include the following:

- Stress is reduced if they do not have to think about handwriting.
- They can be taught to use spell and grammar checks at the end of a piece of writing.
- They can reorganise their ideas quickly and easily, adding ideas, moving things around and editing for improvement.
- Presentation ceases to be a source of worry.
- Motivation increases.

For very dyslexic learners, speech activated software can be useful, but it is not generally allowed in public examinations so children should not become entirely dependent on it. Those who use laptops as part of their daily learning routines can generally use them in exams too.

Aspect 5: Writing – handwriting, punctuation, sentences and text

Letters	Handwriting and punctuation	Sentence structure	Text structure	Content and style	NC level
M	Accurate and consistent letter formation and sizing	Grammatical agreements between pronouns and verbs reflect standard English	Organisation of ideas in non-fiction texts is sensible, with related points close together	Additional detail is given to make a character or setting come alive	3
M	End of sentence punctuation (full stop, question mark, exclamation mark) is generally accurate	Uses different sentence structures for different purposes in a text	Paragraphs are sometimes evident	Characters' thoughts and feelings engage the reader	
N	Handwriting is fast, fluent and legible with some evidence of joining	Some sentences begin with subordinate clauses (e.g. starting with *when, because*)	Openings and closings of texts are clearly signalled	Characters' motives are beginning to be clarified	3
N	Uses speech marks, with some related punctuation	Sentences within paragraphs are linked (e.g. by pronouns or adverbials)	The ending of a story is not rushed	Uses the main features, including layout, of non-fiction text types	

The Target Ladders

Suggested activities

Guided writing

Guided writing with a small group of children can be a very powerful way of supporting dyslexic children. The group does not all need to be at the same level for guided writing (unlike guided reading), but they should all share a learning objective (for example, to use the connectives *because, so, but* accurately in writing). For example:

- Introduce the objective and establish the group's prior knowledge.
- Read a short text to the children which exemplifies the objective and discuss what can be learned from the text.
- Introduce an activity which focuses on the learning objective (for example, to join sentence beginnings and endings using the target connectives).
- Complete the activity orally, discussing each choice made.
- Ask pairs of children to suggest other examples, one child scribing on a whiteboard.
- Let children revisit a previous piece of their writing to find opportunities for redrafting (by copying out one or two sentences) and improving, using the learning objective.

Oral language

Use oral work to develop vocabulary and language.

- *Similes and metaphors*: images are ideal for developing vocabulary and creating pithy descriptions.
- *Make a link*: make a collection of apparently unconnected images (for example, *squirrel, iceberg, kettle, swing, banister, armbands, bicycle, axe*). Give one to each child in a group. How many of the other images can a child link to their image? For example, *kettles have round holes and the valve in an armband has a round hole; the kettle's lead is long like the rope holding up the swing seat*; and so on.
- *Alliterative animal alphabet*: work together to make an alphabet of animal adjectives and nouns (*annoying aardvarks; boring bears;* and so on) or try the extended version with short clauses (*orange octopi organising orang-utans; prancing penguins playing the piano*).
- *Never-ending story*: tell a group story with each person ending their contribution with a connective.
- *Change it around*: explore the impact of fronting clauses in a complex sentence. For example, *At the beginning of the day, Mai broke her finger because she was cross. Mai broke her finger at the beginning of the day because she was cross. Because she was cross at the beginning of the day, Mai broke her finger.*
- *Drop in a clause*: drop a relative clause into a sentence. For example, *The old policeman leaned against the crumbling wall* might become: *The old policeman, whose legs were tired, leaned against the crumbling wall which was covered in ancient ivy.*

Aspect 6: Planning, organising and remembering

Letters	Visual sequencing and memory	Verbal sequencing and memory	Planning	Organising
A	Uses picture sequence to go to the toilet	Follows verbal explanations of picture sequences	Copies adult as adult prepares resources	Follows regular personal routines
A	Uses picture sequence to get dressed	Joins in with singing simple songs and rhymes	Participates in role-play about planning events	Participates in role-play about organising events
B	Uses Now and Next boards to know what will happen next	Understands language *now* and *next*	Collects resources, one thing at a time	Joins an adult in a familiar routine (e.g. putting something away)
B	Sequences two pictures to show 'first' and 'last'	Understands language *first* and *last*		Follows daily classroom routines
C	Uses graphic labels to put resources away	Follows two simple instructions in order (e.g. *Pick up the pencil and sit down*)	Follows prompts to put resources back in the right place	
C	Re-orders three pictures to re-create a familiar personal sequence	Remembers a sequence of three numbers or things	Contributes ideas to role-plays about planning events	Contributes ideas to role-plays about organising events
D	Uses simple chart to collect items for activity	Retells simple familiar stories in sequence	With support, can set a goal or realistic target to achieve immediately	'Re-reads' own role-play writing
D	Continues a visual pattern with two elements (e.g. *red blue red blue red* …)	Rote counts to 10		Plays turn-taking games without support

80   *The Target Ladders*

Suggested activities

Now and Next board

- Use a Now and Next board (or a Now, Next and Later board) to allow the child to understand the structure of events. Otherwise, transitions can become very scary.
  - A Now and Next board has two spaces, each with a strip of Velcro, the first labelled 'Now' and the second 'Next'. Write the words in different colours so the child learns to recognise the colour as much as the word.
  - The board has symbols or photographs featuring all of the different activities the child generally does.
- At the beginning of each new activity, sit with the child and help them to put the appropriate symbol or photograph into its place, emphasising the words 'Now' and 'Next' as you do so. Photographs can seem like the better option because they are individualised and show the actual activities the child will engage with. However, literal children find photographs harder because they may look for the precise configuration of objects in the photograph. Make your choice based on knowledge of the child you are working with.

Tidying up

This is an important part of the school day and there is no reason why a dyslexic child should not participate, as long as they do not have to read.

- Use pictures of the items in the place where they should be put, or cut-out silhouettes for objects which live on surfaces.
- Use colour coding so that, for example, maths resources go in yellow trays and stationery in green ones.
- Keep instructional language as simple and as consistent as possible.

Remembering sequences

Before children will remember sequences in everyday contexts, they will need to learn them in isolation through games and activities.

- *Version 1 of Kim's game*: put three objects in a line on a tray, ask the child to look at it, then close their eyes. Take one object away. Can the child tell you what has been taken away and where in the sequence it went?
- *Version 2 of Kim's game*: place the three objects in a line. When the child has their eyes shut, reorganise the objects. Can the child sequence them again?
- *Silly sequences*: give two instructions to a small world toy and ask the child if the instructions are in a sensible order. If they are, the child should make the toy do what you said; if they are not, the child should say so.
- *I went shopping and I bought*: play versions of this familiar game. Versions can be linked to any topic you are studying: *In the morning the vet saw ...; On the way home I passed ...* . When you play, ask each child who contributes an object to stand in a line. This will give the dyslexic child a better chance of remembering because they can associate the object and the person.

Re-reading mark-making

It is good practice to encourage children to understand, from the beginning, that:

- they should know what they plan to write before they write it;
- when they have finished writing, the writing should 'say' what they planned for it to say.

Establish an expectation that children know what they have written (within the past few minutes) and can read it back to you.

Aspect 6: Planning, organising and remembering

Letters	Visual sequencing and memory	Verbal sequencing and memory	Planning	Organising
E	Remembers, and reproduces from memory, a sequence of three images	Recognises if two instructions are given in a sensible order or not (e.g. *Put on your shoes then put on your socks*)	Collects more than one resource for a familiar activity	Follows regular classroom routines
E	Uses a visual timetable to know what is happening next	Understands language *later* and *soon*		Adds events to visual timetable
F	Sequences personal photos, commenting on changes	Uses language to describe change	Counts number of 'sleeps' until an event happens	Learns some language for meta-cognitive skills
F	Reproduces from memory a sequence of three abstract symbols	Recites the alphabet from memory	With support, can set a goal or realistic target to achieve today	Prioritises between two actions
G	Continues a visual pattern with three elements (e.g. *red blue green red blue green red ...*)	Retells a simple familiar story, listing events in order	Contributes ideas when problem solving for a character in a story	Creates a 'to do' list for a simple activity
G	Reproduces from memory a sequence of four letters, numbers or symbols	Understands language *today, tomorrow, next week, next year*		Uses a timer to understand when an activity needs to start or finish
H	Uses visual checklists independently	Describes or writes step-by-step instructions	Independently puts resources back in the right place	Uses visual checklists effectively
H	Uses visual timetable			Uses visual timetable to collect/carry resources needed

Suggested activities

Visual timetables

Many children in school are supported by visual timetables, which show – in order – all of the lesson or structural activities of the day. The detail into which you go will depend on the age of the children you are working with: a 5-year-old may need to include 'register' and 'toilet time' whereas a 15-year-old just needs to know what the subjects are and when the breaks are. Visual timetables give a shape to the day, so transitions between lessons or activities are much less threatening; instructions are more predictable; concentration increases as anxiety decreases.

If you are planning to make your own visual timetables, try the following:

- Download symbols for visual timetables from the internet. A wide variety of different timetables are available for children of all ages. Or you can buy CDs containing hundreds of symbols from commercial publishers.
- Laminate the symbols and baseboard and stick Velcro dots on each.
- Provide a pouch to keep the symbols together and hang it near the timetable.

Online stores include sellers who make and sell visual timetables, which are already laminated, with Velcro dots.

Language for learning

As children become better learners, they need to develop a vocabulary for talking about learning and themselves as learners. Research suggests that IQ does not change a great deal as we grow older, but we can all improve as learners by learning how to learn more effectively.

- By developing a vocabulary and language to talk about their learning, learning to learn children can:
  ○ identify and build on their strengths;
  ○ learn strategies to overcome barriers;
  ○ understand learning objectives;
  ○ know what 'high-quality learning' is and whether or not they are doing it;
  ○ develop self-confidence and become more motivated to succeed;
  ○ understand their health and the need for nutrition, water, sleep;
  ○ know how to use their teacher's marking to improve their performance;
  ○ identify the strategies which help them most from all of the strategies you teach them;
  ○ take responsibility for improving their learning through reflection, trying new strategies, learning from what went well and what didn't.

Working memory

Working memory is described as the ability to hold in mind and mentally manipulate information over short periods of time. We use our working memory to solve mental arithmetic problems; to blend the sounds in a word or to segment a word; to remember the whole sentence while we work out how to spell one word; to remember what has just happened in a story while we read on to find out what happens next ... we use working memory across the entire school curriculum and into adulthood.

Dyslexic children often have limited working memories. We can support them in various ways:

- Reduce the memory demands on the child. For example, provide recording buttons so that children can record their sentence before trying to write it. The button remembers the sentence while the child works out the spellings.
- Repeat instructions and information as often as necessary – without getting frustrated.
- Break down tasks into manageable chunks.
- Make explicit links to known facts to help the child link new and known information.
- Encourage the use of whiteboards, laptops, scribble pads – anything that reduces the memory load.

Aspect 6: Planning, organising and remembering

Letters	Visual sequencing and memory	Verbal sequencing and memory	Planning	Organising
I		Understands language *yesterday, last week, last year*	With help, begins to split tasks into stages	Is developing an understanding of time
I		Recites the months of the year in order	Says number of days until an event happens	Begins to estimate how long a task will take
J	Sequences numbers to 100	Repeats instructions, having listened to a class introduction	Can set a goal or realistic target to achieve today	Prioritises three actions
J	Spells longer words by remembering the spelling of each syllable	Follows classroom instructions to complete a three-step task appropriately	With support, breaks complex tasks into smaller, achievable tasks	Discusses pros and cons of three actions
K	Uses colour coding to help to sort resources	Story retelling is balanced and clear		Uses weekly planner to organise homework/ projects
K	Puts three numbers up to 100 in order and says the number before and after each one	Identifies the 'main idea' of 5 minutes of teacher talk	Negotiates a solution to a problem	Takes responsibility for own actions
L	Follows a simple map or plan to find something	Summarises the information in a text, retaining order	Can set a goal or realistic target to achieve within the next few weeks	Can 'show what they know' to help others to organise events
L			Breaks complex tasks into smaller, achievable tasks	Evaluates and prioritises tasks to achieve

84   *The Target Ladders*

© *Target Ladders: Dyslexia*   LDA   Permission to Photocopy

Suggested activities

Strategies for remembering

We all use different strategies for remembering information – and your dyslexic child may need to practise a wide range of them before finding those that work best. Try teaching these strategies:

- *Chunking*: we tend to remember phone numbers by saying two strings of about five numbers each rather than one string of ten numbers. Teach this strategy for remembering lists of numbers, nouns, verbs, dates, and so on.
- *Making links*: make explicit links between what you are learning and what you have already learned or experienced.
- *Graphic organisers*: teach children to use charts, diagrams, mind maps and so on to record information.
- *Visualisation*: encourage children to make pictures in their heads while you are speaking. If you are teaching a life cycle, ask children to visualise each aspect of it; if you are teaching spelling, write the word and ask the children to look carefully, then to close their eyes, look up and left and 'see' the word on the inside of their eyelids.
- *Association*: learn new vocabulary by writing definitions and synonyms; learn the months of the year by associating each month with a symbol and remembering the symbols.
- *Word play* (*for example, rhyming, mnemonics, acronyms*): introduce children to these ways of remembering lists, facts, spellings and so on. There are some they can learn, but they will remember best those they work at and make up themselves.

Taking responsibility

Many, many dyslexic people have been successful – but they have taken responsibility for themselves and their learning.

- Dyslexic children need to learn to take responsibility for remembering, sequencing, planning and organising themselves. The teacher's job in helping the children is to introduce the strategies and to gradually increase the expectation. But in the end each child has to learn how to manage themselves. We can help them by:
  ○ teaching them to use planners, calendars and diaries;
  ○ providing supportive learning aids;
  ○ making time for them to record what needs to be done;
  ○ helping them to prioritise and organise by modelling and scaffolding tasks;
  ○ supporting them in setting and achieving their goals.

Learning with the whole class

- Dyslexic children often find it difficult to pay attention, to listen and to learn in whole-class situations. You can help by:
  ○ creating recording sheets so that children have to listen and insert information into the relevant boxes;
  ○ 'chunking information' to enable children to record it on a mind map;
  ○ providing regular summaries of the main points during the lesson;
  ○ breaking up a teaching session with opportunities for children to clarify what they have learned with a response partner;
  ○ offering opportunities for the child to repeat the main points to an adult immediately after the teacher talk.

Aspect 6: Planning, organising and remembering

Letters	Visual sequencing and memory	Verbal sequencing and memory	Planning	Organising
M	Follows algorithms in maths to solve problems with more than one step	Follows instructions without visual reminders	Answers own question: *'what do I have to do?'* and begins a task	Answers own question: *what resources do I need?'*, finds resources and begins the task
M	Can explain the sequence of events in a short film	Participates in school council, or other activity, asking questions and offering ideas	Reads a calendar	Uses ICT effectively (e.g. electronic spell checker, calculator)
N	Uses a mind map to record key ideas while teacher is talking	Talks easily in past, present and future tenses	Takes pride in a task, without the need for recognition	Has correct equipment to hand in all lessons
N	Uses mind mapping or other techniques to record ideas and plans	Can articulate what is needed and knows the order in which to tackle tasks	Uses a diary to plan ahead	Recognises what needs to be done and organises self and others to achieve it

The Target Ladders

© *Target Ladders: Dyslexia*   LDA   Permission to Photocopy

Suggested activities

Following algorithms and remembering equations and formulae

Since sequencing is challenging for young dyslexics, algorithms, which generally involve a sequence of ideas, can be very challenging. Use ideas for developing working memory (pp. 32–3) to support children in learning and using the algorithms and teach them these strategies:

- *Repetition*: repeating something over and over again helps to retain it in your short-term memory. Revisiting it frequently during that day, and the next, then less often over the next week, and once or twice over the following months, will help to secure it in the long-term memory.
- *Use*: we all know that skills that you learn and then do not use are forgotten. Give frequent opportunities to use the algorithm.
- *Record it*: before children start to do a calculation based on a formula, ask them to record the formula. Otherwise the overload on working memory is likely to mean that the attempt is unsuccessful.

Asking questions

Once children are beginning to learn from listening, they can begin to develop roles on the school council and take part in activities in which they need to be able to listen to what others are saying and prepare to ask questions and offer opinions that build on what has been said by others.

- If children are used to recording while they listen, encourage them to use this strategy in all forums where they need to listen.
- Teach the children how to disagree politely with what someone has said and put an alternative position.
- Model dealing with someone who disagrees with what you have said. Talk about how you can do this without getting angry.
- Once children can agree and disagree with each other, develop the skill of listening and asking questions. The questions should be intended to challenge or clarify what the speaker has already said.
- Give children practice in class at listening to each other and making a comment or asking a question. Activities such as circle time and speaking and listening sessions are ideal for this.

Real opportunities for planning

Involve your dyslexic children in planning for real events.

- Daily events.
  - Give the child a visual timetable and expect them to have the appropriate resources at the beginning of each lesson.
  - Provide a list of resources which are needed for maths each day and expect the child to organise the resources for their own table.
  - Let children take responsibility for organising photocopying. Expect them to take a message and the hard copy to the office. Establish expectations of good behaviour as they do it.
- Weekly events, such as spelling tests, need to be managed too.
  - Dyslexic children can be responsible for distributing and collecting books or papers.
  - Give children responsibility for setting up and clearing up after different types of assembly or school clubs.
- Annual and special events. Make sure that your dyslexic children are included in planning for school fairs, productions and so on.

Make opportunities for the children to talk to adults before their planned events and to make lists of equipment and resources necessary. The more often children participate in planning and organising, the better they will engage with it.

Aspect 7: Self-confidence and motivation

Letters	Self-confidence	Behaviours for learning	Interest and motivation	Attention and concentration
A	Names feelings (*happy, sad*) and demonstrates awareness of what they mean	Decides between two activity choices	Seems to be happy/have fun in school at least once a week	With support, can pay attention on a self-chosen activity for up to 2 minutes
A	Identifies something or someone that makes them feel happy	Makes brief eye contact when being addressed	Attempts to join in group singing/storytelling activities	Remains in a self-chosen place for 2 minutes
B	Can say if a character is '*kind*' or '*bad*' in a familiar story	Talks to, or communicates with, at least one person in the class	With support, will participate in oral activities	Uses Now and Next boards to know what will happen next
B	Through role-play, demonstrates understanding of the link between a character's feelings and an action	Uses a choice-board with up to six activity choices	Shows interest in stories	Can 'wait a minute' before needs are met
C	Names feelings (*excited, proud, friendly*) and demonstrates awareness of what they mean	Answers the register appropriately	Sits quietly when a story is being read	Follows two simple instructions in order (e.g. *Pick up the pencil and sit down*)
C	Says something they think they are good at	Follows classroom routines for entering the room		Concentrates for 2 minutes at self-directed activities
D	Says what they like doing	With support, can set a goal or realistic target to achieve immediately	Participates in oral activities independently	With support, can use a timer to sustain concentration for 4 minutes
D	Says what they dislike doing	Seeks support from an adult when there's a difficulty	Begins tasks when requested	Follows an instruction directed at the whole class

The Target Ladders

Suggested activities

Look after yourself and other adults in the classroom

In order to provide appropriate support for children who have poor self-esteem, confidence, attention and concentration, you need to make sure that you are emotionally sufficiently resilient.

- *Try to keep things in perspective*. Remember that the child is not being difficult to upset you: it is part of their learning difficulty.
- *Choose your battles*. One of the advantages of setting targets is that you have prioritised the most important areas for development, so you can tactically ignore some other areas.
- *Believe in the child*. Trust that a dyslexic child can and will mature, grow and achieve. It may take lots of small steps and setbacks but, with your help, they will improve.
- *Support each other*. Other colleagues in your school will also be working with dyslexic children who may display other learning, social or emotional behaviours. Offer each other emotional support.
- *Find out more*. The more you understand dyslexia, the better you will understand the child. Visit www.bdadyslexia.org.uk or www.beingdyslexic.co.uk for more information or read books such as *How to Identify and Support Children with Dyslexia* by Chris Neanon (LDA, 2002).

Supporting children with attention problems

Talk to the child about the fact that they do not concentrate for as long as other children in the class. Help them to talk about what they find easy and difficult about paying attention. (Try a solution-focused approach: see page 95.) Attention is developmental, so immature children may not be able to pay attention as well as, or for as long as, their peers.

- *Allow for regular movement and breaks*. If you allow them, then you are maintaining control of the expectations. Do not allow the child to take unauthorised brain breaks.
- *Use signals*. Agree signals or visual prompts with the child which you can use when you think they may be off-task.
- *Try physical supports* such as air cushions or weighted lap or shoulder wraps. These are often recommended for children with ADHD.
- *Follow the child's interests*. Children will generally concentrate better when they are interested. Try to find out what interests them and use it as the basis for some work tasks.
- *Minimise distractions*. Individual work spaces or privacy boards can be personalised with visual timetables, word lists, stickers and so on and can help to minimise the child's awareness of other children in the classroom.
- *Develop planning skills*. Whether the child plans in words, in pictures or in writing, ask them to plan the one or two steps they will need to take to achieve an immediate goal.
- *Avoid using breaks as a reward*. Rewards such as 'you can go out to play when you have ...' encourage work habits that are quick and careless and demonstrate to the child that these are acceptable.

Using timers

Use timers to encourage high-quality work by the simple expedient of putting them over on their side when the work is not being done to your satisfaction and turning them back again when the child starts to work as you have asked.

- Initially, keep expectations of focused time working to a minimum, with a clear and desirable reward.
- Make expectations and sanctions clear.

Congratulate the child when they have achieved their target even if there have been lots of time outs.

Aspect 7: Self-confidence and motivation

Letters	Self-confidence	Behaviours for learning	Interest and motivation	Attention and concentration
E	Accepts praise without making a fuss	Identifies the 'right choice' in role-play	Has fun with friends	Will stay in one place for up to 5 minutes at a teacher-directed activity
E	Tells someone what they did that was good	Puts up hand to answer closed or yes/no questions	Brings in objects from home to show interests	Plays turn-taking games without support
F	Says things they think they are better at than other people	Can break a simple, short-term goal down into two or three achievable steps	Uses a visual timetable to know what is happening next	Perseveres for a minute if something goes wrong
F	Predicts how an adult will respond to something they have achieved	With support, can identify what happened when they did not make a good choice	Compares two activities in school and says which is better and why	Can wait for more than 1 minute for wants to be met
G	With some support, identifies characters in books who are/are not *lonely, loved, cared for, happy, belonging, friendly*	With support, can set a goal or realistic target to achieve today	Politely accepts an offer of help from an adult	Can handle more than one thing happening at a time
G	Can say positive things about some other people in the group	Evaluates progress towards the goal	Shows interest in collecting rewards for good work or behaviour	Uses a fiddle toy to sustain concentration when teacher is talking
H	Contributes positive comments to self-evaluation activities	Gets on well with most children in the class	Talks about changes that might help them to be more interested	Talks about changes that might help them to pay better attention
H	Suggests things to include in lists of 'What I am good at'	Participates in circle time/SEAL games and discussions	Resists the temptation to join another child's unwanted behaviour	Uses a timer to understand when an activity needs to start or finish

Suggested activities

Accepting praise

For children with very low self-esteem, accepting praise is very worrying as it challenges the children's understanding of themselves. For this reason, some children will reject the praise, destroy the piece of work that has been praised or show inappropriate behaviours in order to attract your disapproval. For these children you can try approaches such as the following:

- Use a stamp or sticker in their books, to make it clear that you are commenting on the work, not on them.
- Make all praise very explicit, so the child knows what they have done well.
- Offer the praise quietly and individually. Many children will accept praise on a one-to-one basis that they will not accept more publicly.
- Ask the child to identify their best picture, the letter *e* that they formed most neatly, or the best piece of writing, so that they have some control over what is praised.

Projecting 'self'

Do a class project on 'self' which focuses on developing self-esteem.

- Pass round a box with a mirror in the bottom. Tell the children that they are to peep inside to see something amazing, wonderful and important. Warn them not to tell anyone else what they saw.
- Ask children to draw self-portraits of themselves being good at something, dreaming about something, being sad about something …
- Let each child make their own time capsule which includes their handprint, footprint, digital photo, family photo, picture of their favourite food, any pets, lists of best films, favourite books, best friends …
- Let children use different colours of sand, chalk and salt to make a feelings jar.

Making choices

To a large extent, children's behaviours can be controlled and pitfalls avoided. For this to happen, children need to learn to recognise their feelings and to make choices about whether or not they act on them: experiencing difficult feelings is fine; acting on them is not. Giving children clear choices, while they are still calm, tells them what the correct behaviour is and also makes it clear that their behaviour is their choice.

- Use the language of choice whenever you feel that the child is becoming out of control: *'You have two choices. Either you can choose to finish the work now, or you can sit on the time out chair for […] minutes and do the work after that. Can you make a good choice?'*.
- Be consistent in the language you use.
- Follow through on all consequences.
- Congratulate a child for making the good choice.
- If they make the bad choice, use role-play, puppets, small world characters or stories to follow up and explore what might have happened if they had made the right choice.

Using fiddle toys

Many adults find it hard to sustain listening without doodling, writing or wriggling. Most children with attention difficulties also find it hard. They will fiddle with Velcro straps on their shoes, the carpet, a book, someone else's hair … However, if you provide a fiddle toy:

- The child is fiddling with something with your permission rather than without it.
- You retain control over when they have access to the toy.
- It can aid concentration in children who cannot concentrate without movement.
- It can relieve stress.

Aspect 7: Self-confidence and motivation

Letters	Self-confidence	Behaviours for learning	Interest and motivation	Attention and concentration
I	Suggests things to include in lists of 'What I am not good at'	Can say 'no' to another child	Asks for help in a confident and clear manner	Uses visual timetable to collect/carry resources needed
I	Accurately identifies things they are good at and things they are less good at	With help, begins to split tasks into stages	Identifies what they would like to happen in school	Maintains focus on a task for 10 minutes
J	Names feelings (*surprised*, *hopeful*, *disappointed*, *scared*) and demonstrates understanding of what they mean	Responds appropriately when told off	Has energy to complete most tasks	Resists some distractions for 5 minutes
J	Says positive things about most other people in the group	Sets a goal or realistic target to achieve today	Often seems to be happy in school	Follows classroom instructions to complete a three-step task appropriately
K	Names feelings (*worried*, *relaxed*, *proud*, *determined*, *bored*, *frustrated*) and talks about body language shown for each emotion	Takes responsibility for own actions	Is willing to share worries with an adult	Maintains focus on a task for 15 minutes
K	With some help, can draw, act or describe feelings of a fictional character	Puts up hand to answer open questions	Seeks attention from the teacher only when appropriate	Generally produces tidy work, at a reasonable pace
L	Understands and illustrates from own experience emotions (*confused*, *guilty*, *embarrassed*, *wary*)	Is not afraid of new things or taking on new tasks	Depends on themselves to get things done	Shows determination to complete a task
L	Shows resilience when identifying what has gone wrong	Can set a goal or realistic target to achieve within the next few weeks	Predicts where the obstacles might be and suggests ideas to overcome them	Is actively involved in activities within the classroom

Suggested activities

Developing emotional literacy

Before children take control of the range of emotions they feel, they need to learn to name and identify the emotions.

- Use picture cards, or print images from the internet, of people showing feelings using body language. Ask children to name the feelings. Play feelings bingo with feelings the children are familiar with.
- Talk about '*what makes me feel [angry, frustrated, confident, happy, determined]*.' Record the scenarios for role-play at a later point.
- Talk about '*What I do and say when I feel ...*'
- Take photos of the children expressing the emotions. Talk about their body language and facial expressions.
- When you read to or with the children, ask them to make links between the characters' responses to events and the emotions you have been talking about.

Personal power

Children with a sense of personal power are those who are able to take responsibility for their actions because they recognise that it is in their own power to change how they are and to make an impact on the world around them. They can change things about themselves and their immediate surroundings that they don't like; they can learn; they can cope; they have self-assertiveness and are able to engage in self-appraisal.

- Make fish shapes out of coloured paper. Distribute a handful of these to each child and ask them to record (or ask someone else to record) each time they solve a problem or do something they have not done before.
- As the children give you the fish, use them to make an '*I can solve problems*' frieze, or put them in a piece of netting to make an '*I can solve problems*' display.

Developing concentration

Run a concentration group.

- Begin each session with a welcome discussion, in which everybody talks about triumphs or difficulties from the week.
- Move into a colouring activity where the children colour squares neatly, using a different colour for each square. Begin with 10 seconds of colouring followed by a 30 second break until children have achieved one minute of colouring.
  - Build up session by session until the children are colouring for 30 seconds with a 10-second break.
  - At the end of each colouring activity, ask children to count the total number of squares coloured and write it down. How does it change over time?
- Put out a variety of different 3-minute activities: have a mixture of 'fun activities' (for example, construction, jigsaws, marble run, skittles) and 'school activities' (for example, tracing, mental maths, copying words). Rotate around the activities. The aim is that each child is trying to focus on what they need to do without looking to see what the others are doing. Record how many of each of the 'school' activities the child achieves in a week.
  - For older children, it may be more appropriate to put out a number of PE activities (basketball hoops, skipping ropes, aiming) as well as a few 'school' activities.
- Have a finishing session in which children talk about what they have achieved this session. Ask children to talk about their experiences of trying to concentrate when other things are happening. What helps children to concentrate or makes it harder?
- Over six weeks, how much have the children's scores in the colouring and 'school activities' increased?
- How much has their awareness of what helps them to concentrate grown? Talk to them about the implications of this awareness for their work in the classroom.

Aspect 7: Self-confidence and motivation

Aspect 7: Self-confidence and motivation

Letters	Self-confidence	Behaviours for learning	Interest and motivation	Attention and concentration
M	Has friends among their peers, and is not a loner	Works collaboratively with others and is an effective communicator in group discussions	Works independently unless a problem arises that cannot be solved without the teacher's help	Perseveres with tasks, even when they are challenging
M	Is confident in most situations	Makes a good behaviour choice even when it is hard	Generally gets enjoyment from school tasks and consequently completes them without complaint	Is determined to complete an unwelcome task
N	Is able to think confidently about differences between self and others	Seems to have a good grasp of how to organise learning tasks so that they can be successfully completed	Gets started on tasks without delay and has the motivation to carry them through	Manages to work when others around them are talking at a reasonable level
N	Accurately and calmly identifies things they are good at and things they are less good at	Accommodates easily to changes in routine and different people	Shows an interest in most schoolwork	Is attentive, listens to the teacher and is not easily distracted from the task in hand

The Target Ladders

Suggested activities

Solution-focused approach

Try a solution-focused approach to increasing confidence and motivation. A session for a solution-focused approach might include:

Focus on the positive

- Talk about the good things: what has gone well; what the child is proud of having achieved; what makes them feel good.

Talk about exceptions to feeling negative about literacy

- Can the child think of any occasion when they managed to read or write without difficulty? It could be something like reading or writing in a birthday card, reading information in a game of Top Trumps, sharing a comic, writing a message or a list.
- Talk about what is different about the occasion when reading/writing felt OK.
- Encourage the child to produce the answers and think about what they did, what the task required, who else was involved, how much they wanted to participate, and so on.

Identify a goal and scale it

- From this conversation, can the child identify their own immediate goal?
- If not, develop the conversation and listen to what the child is saying about what they can and cannot do in reading and writing.
- Agree what a good goal would be.
- Draw a line from 1 to 10, where 10 is achieving the goal and doing it easily and well, and 0 is nowhere near it, can't do it, it's too hard.
- Ask the child to tell you where on the line they think they are now.
- Can they also identify where they think they would need to get to in order to feel OK about this aspect of their learning?
- If the child scales themselves now more than one or two points below where they think they would like to be, revisit the goal and simplify it. The idea is to achieve the goal.

Agree what it would look and feel like to achieve the goal.

- Use the magic wand test: 'If I waved a magic wand so you could achieve the goal …'
  - How would you know you had done it?
  - Who else would know?
  - How would they know?
  - How would you know they knew?
- Use discussions arising from the questions to encourage the child to describe the situation they would like to see.

This, then, is the long-term goal, but now the child has defined it and understands what it would look and feel like.

Finish the session

Finish the session on a positive note:

- Congratulate the child on something they have done or said in the course of the session – and be explicit about what they have done or said and why you are pleased.
- Agree specific tasks for the child to do between this session and the next one. The tasks should relate closely to the child's goal and their response to the magic wand question.

There are a variety of books that can give you more information on using a solution-focused approach, including: John Rhodes and Yasmin Ajmal, *Solution Focused Thinking in Schools: Behaviour, Reading and Organisation* (BT Press, 1995).

Links to other *Target Ladders* titles

Other books in the Differentiating for Inclusion series may well include targets which will be appropriate for some dyslexic learners. For example:

Target Ladders: Autistic Spectrum
Louise Nelson

Includes additional targets for:
- Personal organisation
- Getting attention
- Social interaction
- Managing feelings

Target Ladders: Behavioural, Emotional and Social Difficulties
Rachel Foulger, Sue Smallwood and Marion Aust

Includes additional targets for:
- Controlling emotions
- Managing transitions
- Taking responsibility
- Social interaction

Target Ladders: Speech, Language and Communication Needs
Susan Lyon et al.

Includes additional targets for:
- Attention control
- Comprehension
- Social communication
- Pragmatic understanding

Other useful resources from LDA

How to Identify and Support Children with Dyslexia
Chris Neanon

Dyslexia in the Open: A toolkit for building self-esteem
Wonnie Barry and Sally Nimmo

Beat Dyslexia: A step-by-step multi-sensory literacy programme (Books 1–6)
Elizabeth Franks, Myra Nicholson and Celia Stone

Stile Dyslexia (Books 1–10)
Shireen Shuster

A specially structured self-checking programme to take pupils through the rules of spelling and grammar using a phonic approach. Use with *Stile Tray*.

How to Develop Numeracy in Children with Dyslexia
Pauline Clayton

ACE Spelling Dictionary
David Moseley

A unique approach in which pupils need only think how a word sounds to find how to spell it; this is a favourite for improving dyslexics' spelling.